Ten Evenings
With God

Ten Evenings With God

Ilia Delio, OSF

Liguori
LIGUORI, MISSOURI

Imprimi Potest:
Thomas D. Picton, CSsR • Provincial, Denver Province • The Redemptorists

Published by Liguori Publications • Liguori, Missouri • www.liguori.org

Library of Congress Cataloging-in-Publication Data
Delio, Ilia.
    Ten evenings with God / Ilia Delio.
        p. cm.
    Includes bibliographical references.
    ISBN 978-0-7648-1742-7
    1. Spirituality. 2. Spiritual life—Christianity. I. Title. II.
Title: Ten evenings with God.
    BV4501.3.D446 2008
269'.6—dc22   2008016448

Liguori Publications, a nonprofit corporation, is an apostolate of the Redemptorists. To learn more about the Redemptorists, visit Redemptorists.com.

Printed in the United States of America
15 14 13 12 11 / 6 5 4 3 2
First edition

A book comes into being, that is, becomes a book, not simply with the ideas of an author but with the reading of the text. Every reading of the text helps create the book. This is true for all books both large and small, and it is particularly true for this one. I am grateful to the following people who read *Ten Evenings With God* and offered their comments: Stephen Kluge, O.F.M., Dr. Kenneth Harrington, and Dr. Thelma Steiger. I am particularly grateful to Sister Kate Murphy, O.S.F., who read the book, offered her comments, and challenged me on a few points. At the age of ninety-plus Kate continues to seek the will of God and still has a number of questions about God. I was thoroughly delighted to receive Kate's comments and to know that even in the senior years of life, God always remains an incomprehensible mystery of love, luring us, desiring us, and embracing us, as we "wonder our way" into the glory of eternal life.

ILIA DELIO, OSF

Contents

Introduction

Happiness and freedom are the two main desires of the
human heart. Every person desires to be happy, and by this I mean
every person wants to be loved, to feel secure, to be at peace, and
to experience goodness. But every person also desires freedom, to
live without coercion or constraint, spontaneously alive in choice
and action. This concept of freedom, however, is the secular view,
the worldly idea of freedom as the ability to choose for oneself, as
the idol of my parents' generation, Frank Sinatra, once sang, "I Did
It My Way."

The worldly idea of freedom fits snugly into the consumer culture in which we are immersed with its preferred promises of en-
during happiness, beauty, and longevity. Larger homes, bigger cars,
luxury upon luxury—we are led to believe that happiness is having
everything we want and freedom is the ability to attain our desires.
This may work for some people who are skillful in accumulating
wealth, but the truth is real happiness and freedom have little to do
with material things or living without constraint—and everything
to do with God, who is the source of all that exists.

Some people come to realize the truth of happiness and freedom
only when they can no longer depend on material things to fulfill
their thirst for life's deepest desires, such as when illness strikes or
they lose a loved one or a natural disaster destroys all their possessions. Others never find happiness or freedom because they are too
enmeshed in themselves and enslaved by their personal desires. But
for those who are willing to walk by faith, happiness and freedom
can be found by seeking the will of God.

Although many books (including many based on the insights of Saint Ignatius of Loyola, the great teacher of spiritual discernment) address the subject of the will of God, I have chosen to explore the will of God not as end in itself but as the path to freedom, not the freedom of autonomy but the freedom to love. Too often these days, especially in the public political sector, we find "will of God" language used as a trump card for political agendas whether they entail stem-cell research, euthanasia, or the war in the Middle East. The politicizing of the will of God amid material wealth has created confusion and fragmentation in society—leading either to an abandonment of God or a shallow understanding of the will of God.

For some, the will of God is unimportant; for others, it is a fearful force that defines life. As a result, many young people have difficulty discerning their vocation in life. Amid life's confusion they ask, "What is God's will for me?" For some, the will of God seems too vague and obscure and so they exchange it for accumulated wealth (happiness is creating your own heaven on earth). For others, the will of God requires certainty and so they are drawn to institutions of rigid, hierarchical structure where the principal virtue is blind obedience. However, neither abandoning the will of God nor forming it into an ideology leads to freedom and happiness; rather, either extreme can easily throw one into despair and confusion.

The will of God will always elude us if we are looking for certainty. Because we live in a scientific age, we contemporary folk prefer immediate answers with a high degree of certitude. Just as science provides us with data, so too, we want God to be explicit about the divine plans for us. Perhaps this desire for certainty is not too different from the ancient Israelites who wandered in the desert and got lost. When Moses returned from Mount Sinai with the Ten Commandments, he found the Israelites had begun worshipping an idol—a god they could see and control. Moses returned to the mountain to ask God for more explicit directions, more concrete revelation, and visible presence. But God said to him, "[W]hile my glory passes by I will put you in a cleft of the rock, and I will cover you with my hand until I have passed by; then I will take away my hand, and you shall see my back; but my face shall not be seen" (Exodus 33:22-23). God revealed to Moses that Divine Presence is always hidden; one cannot see the face of God and live. That is because God is much more than we can imagine or conceive. We can never really know God or God's ways because God is beyond all knowledge; God is incomprehensible love.

Yet, while the amazing mystery of God is beyond our human comprehension, it is not out of our spiritual reach. In his classic autobiography, Saint Augustine (of Hippo) tells us that he searched everywhere for God only to realize that "you were more inward than my inmost self, and superior to my highest being."[1] We are not only capable of knowing God within us (though we may not attain complete knowledge of God), but we are also capable of loving God (which is a higher form of knowledge) and thus we are created to live in the will of God.

In short, the source of our happiness and freedom lies in God when we come to know ourselves in God. To discover our identity is to find God, and to find God is to discover happiness in which lies our freedom. The medieval theologian, Saint Bonaventure, once said that happiness is of the heart. "No one can be made happy," he wrote, "unless he or she rises above oneself by an ascent of the heart. But we cannot rise above ourselves unless a higher power lifts us up." Saint Bonaventure tell us, "Prayer, is the mother and source of the ascent."[2] If we desire happiness, then we must learn to pray because the will of God is not a thing or object to attain, it is not a blueprint but a living relationship of love.

The will of God cannot be purchased for a price or extinguished by oppressive forces, but it is a freedom deep within the human heart. If we find this freedom and live from its source of energy, we will discover the giftedness of our humanity and the freedom to become the human person that God has created us to be.

To explore this relationship between the will of God and freedom, I offer ten evenings of prayerful reflections. In the first evening, the revelation of God as love is discussed as the foundation for the will of God. As you awaken to the presence of God in your life, it is good to ask, "Who is God? How do you experience God?" Once you begin to explore the question of God, you will begin to plumb the depths of the will of God.

On the second evening, we examine prayer as relationship with God, the importance of solitude for listening to God, and the use of the senses in discerning God's presence in our lives. The third evening focuses more specifically on discernment and the meaning of discernment as integral to human life. The fourth evening explores the signs of knowing when our choices are leading us in the right direction or when they are leading us in the wrong direction. Here the insights of Ignatius of Loyola are tapped to distinguish between good and evil spirits and the difference between these spirits.

Ignatius's "intellectual" approach is tempered by an emphasis on the movements of the heart when we look at discernment through the lens of the Franciscan tradition. The Franciscan approach to discernment is attentiveness to the interior movements of the heart. Following Augustine's insight on the restless heart that longs for God, discernment is examined as the heart of God in search of the human heart: Heart calls to heart. Discernment, therefore, is an ongoing movement through a deepening of relationship with God.

Approaching the middle of our ten-day journey, the fifth evening is a time of letting go and coming to realize that living in the will of

God is a continuous growth of wheat among the weeds of our lives. On the sixth evening, we move beyond how to make choices in life to living life as the choice for God. The maturing of discernment is expressed in surrender or the entrusting of oneself to God. It is a deepening of life in God through openness, poverty of being, and receptivity, all of which are the fruit of prayer and the centering of one's life in God. Gratitude becomes the language of surrender when we accept the totality of life as gift.

The seventh and eighth evenings bring us to the realization that living in the will of God is living in the ebb and flow of love. Our tendency in everyday life prompts us to hold on and control the events of our lives, but each moment invites us to let go into God and allow God to be the center of our thoughts and actions. Because we easily forget the simplicity of letting go and allowing God's love to govern our lives, we look to the book of nature to teach us the path to holiness through self-surrender. Thus we take a moment in the eighth evening to consider nature as a mirror of our lives as we seek to find God in the changes of our lives. Nature teaches us that to live in surrender to God is to discover freedom in love, and happiness as the enjoyment of being alive.

The ninth evening reflects on the progression from surrender to freedom, where we experience life in the Spirit of God as being possessed by God. That is, we experience the fidelity of God's love and trust the divine presence to such a degree that our choices in life are for the sake of love alone, a love greater than ourselves but which completes ourselves. Freedom is choosing our path in life that leads to the fullness of love. This is the path of Jesus Christ who shows us the meaning of freedom in love, which is love unto death; that is, freedom in love leads to the cross. The one who lives in surrender to God, and thus freely in God, is not afraid to die but rather sees death as integral to the fullness of life. For such a person true freedom is the path of true commitment where love of the other is greater than love of self.

On the tenth and final evening, we begin to see that by loving the other, a person truly loves oneself because it is in union with the other that one finds oneself. Only when we begin to live in the will of God as the freedom to be ourselves does the unfolding of the reign of God through our lives take place. Christ lives only when we can give ourselves away in love. To live in love is to live in Christ or rather to give birth to Christ in our lives. This is the meaning of Christian love.

The path from prayer to surrender to freedom is the path to life. To seek the will of God is to seek life, to be a human person. The early Church Father, Irenaeus of Lyons, once said that the glory of God is the human person fully alive. This is what we are created for—the glory of God—nothing more and nothing less. Do our lives give God glory? Are we growing in the freedom of love? This small book may not provide any immediate answers but hopefully it will provide fertile soil for the mind and heart so that, like the tiny mustard seed, our lives may grow into a harvest of love.

ILIA DELIO, OSF

First Evening

Awakening and Discovery

Life in God is a daring adventure through the uncharted depths of love. God breathes life into us through the Spirit of love, and this Spirit of love is the daily breath of our lives. We do not belong to God as slaves or fearful creatures but as children of a loving Father, brothers and sisters of Jesus Christ, and spouses of the Holy Spirit. Life with God is relational because God is a Trinity of love. God is not a "loner" or an isolated "thinker." God is not an elderly grandfather or the Marlboro man or an emperor. Rather, "God" is Trinity, a communion of persons in love. Relationship, therefore, is fundamental to what we call the "will of God." In his book *New Seeds of Contemplation,* Thomas Merton highlights relationship as the true meaning of God's will. Too often we think of the will of God as an impersonal law rather than as an invitation to love, he indicates. We think of God's will like a force that controls us rather than an intimate encounter that takes place in contemplation. "We must learn to realize that the love of God seeks us in every situation," he writes, "and seeks our good."[3] To know the will of God is to awaken to God's love within us and around us. It is to realize that we are created out of love, we exist in love, and we are destined for eternal love. If all of creation flows out of love and unto love, then the only reason for our existence is *to love.* To be a Christian is to love well—to love first.

The problem with God is one of utter simplicity. We tend to com-

plicate God by projecting onto God everything we think God is or
should be or might be. The beauty of Jesus Christ is the revelation of
God, summed by the First Letter of John: "God is love" (1 John 4:8).
How simple—*God is love*—and out of this love flows all of life.

Why do we speak of the love of God? Because the will of God
is God's inscrutable love for us! The *will* connotes affectivity and
desire; it is the gravity of being. The will of God is not a "thing" or
a rule or an object to attain. It is not like getting a degree or finding the right spouse. We cannot find the will of God as if finding an
object; nor can we follow the will of God as if following a method
or a plan of life. We cannot understand God's love in the same way
we understand a math problem or a story. The will of God is the
perfect, simple, absolute love of God and the desire of God for his
creatures.

Just as we humans are filled with many desires, fame, wealth,
friendship, happiness, and peace, so too God is filled with desire;
above all, the desire that we love God with our entire being, and in
this love give glory to God. Thus we cannot know the will of God
apart from the love of God and the desire for God. Faith is belief in
the love of God, which is beyond our comprehension because it is
divine love, a love that is eternal, perfect, and immutable.

To seek the will of God is to remain open to the many ways God
expresses his love for us, through our neighbors, our family members, our community, or the beauty of creation. God's love is mystery; it is incomprehensible, ineffable, invisible, indescribable, yet
this love is the reason for our lives and for the life of this universe.
Without the love of God we would not exist.

God's will is God's love for us and we must be ready to encounter that love, accept it, and respond to it in love. The meaning of
our lives can only be found in the love of God. For deep in the love
of God lies our happiness, our peace, our hope, and our fullness of

life. In this first evening, it is enough to ponder the profound simplicity of God: God is Love.

What Is the "Will of God?"

Life presents a series of unending choices. Day by day we are confronted by the need to make decisions, some of which are small decisions and others that can be "life-changing" decisions. How do we know what to decide? If we change jobs or decide to marry or enter a religious community, how do we know that our choice is in accordance with God's will? What if we make the "wrong" choice? Will God punish us? Not too long ago, a young woman I knew decided to leave religious life after a difficult time of trying to live in community. Although she went through the proper channels of discernment, she still wondered about her decision and left saying, "I hope God does not punish me for this!" Many people are beset by the fear of God, as if God is quick to anger and slow to forgive. This may be the image of God portrayed in parts of the Old Testament, but this is not the God revealed in the person of Jesus Christ. The God of Jesus Christ is the God of unconditional love, and we must begin to see the will of God through the eyes of love.

The will of God is God's desire to love each of us unconditionally and freely, as if each person was born for God alone. The will of God is the Spirit of God eternally breathed forth by the mutual love between the Father and the Son. Each of us is created through this continuous act of eternal love; we are created out of God's desire to share love personally and individually. Because God is love, God can "will" nothing less than love, and anything other than love is not the will of God. That is why any disaster or misfortune cannot be the will of God because God does not desire our destruction or annihilation but life for us. Bad things happen to good people not because God "wills" it so but because we are finite beings. All of creation depends on God because everything in creation is created by God. Creation cannot control its own destiny or fate because we are not God—although our trying to "play God" can have disastrous effects on creation.

Recently a deadly tornado struck a small town in Kansas and almost all the residents lost their homes, which were completely ravaged by the storm. Instead of blaming God for the destruction or seeing their misfortune as the will of God, however, many residents came together and prayed in thanksgiving that they were alive and physically unharmed. Because God wills only our good, he can draw good out of situations that otherwise seem completely destructive.

Hope is belief in the goodness of God when everything seems to fail. If we truly believe that God is love and that love never fails, then hope is our anchor to life in times of darkness. In God's will is our hope because God alone can raise what is dead back to life. Even when things go wrong and the world around us falls into a thousand little pieces, God's will is the source of our strength because God's will is God's faithful and abiding love for us.

In his book *He Leadeth Me,* Father Walter Ciszek, a Jesuit priest who was captured during the Second World War and imprisoned for many years in Siberia, came to realize through years of hardship and persecution that God is always present and constant in love. What is fascinating about Father Walter's story, as he describes it, is his growth in understanding the will of God. He began his ministry to Eastern Catholics by answering the call for missionaries to Russia shortly before the outbreak of World War II. He said that his entire goal in life was "to do the will of God," even writing his undergraduate thesis on "obedience to the will of God." He answered the call to go east wholeheartedly by first going to Poland en route to Russia. It was not long after he settled in Poland that he was captured by the Russians.

The capture and imprisonment of Father Walter was the beginning of his journey into the wilderness of life. Only gradually and through much suffering did he come to realize that God's will cannot be accomplished by "self-will"; rather, it is a much deeper expression of the fidelity of God. He wrote:

> *God is constant in his love if we will but look to him, he will sustain us in every storm if we will but cry out to him, he will save us if we will but reach out our hand to him. He is there, if we will only turn to him and learn to trust in him alone. The upheavals in this world, or in the Church herself, are not the end of everything, especially of his love. They can in fact serve best us signs to remind us of his love and of his constancy, to make us turn once more to him and cling to him again when all else that we counted on is overturned around us....Mysteriously, God in his providence must make use of our tragedies to remind our fallen human nature of his presence and his love, of the constancy of his concern and care for us. It is not vindictiveness on his part; he does not send us tragedies to punish us for having so long forgotten him. The failing is on our part. He is always present and ever faithful; it is we who fail to see him or to look for him in times of ease and comfort, to remember he is there, shepherding and guarding and providing us the very things we come to count on and expect to sustain us every day. Yet we fail to remember that, comfortable as we are in our established order and the status quo, as day follows day.[4]*

While Father Walter's journey was an extremely difficult one, he understood that sometimes God allows our whole world to be turned upside down in order to remind us that here on earth we have no lasting home; ultimately we are dependent on God alone.[5]

Hence the words of Jesus on the Mount: [D]o not worry about your life, what you will eat or what you will drink, or about your body, what you will wear. Is not life more than food, and the body more than clothing?...your heavenly Father knows that you need all these things. But strive first for the kingdom of God and his righteousness, and all these things will be given to you as well" (Matthew 6:25-34). Our choice to do the "will of God" is a choice for God alone regardless of the circumstances in which we find ourselves.

Father Walter learned of God's faithfulness only after years of suffering in the frozen plains of Siberia. Yet, once this seed of knowledge took root in his heart, he knew that "that neither death, nor life, nor angels, nor rulers, nor things present, nor things to come, nor powers, nor height, nor depth, nor anything else in all creation, will be able to separate us from the love of God in Christ Jesus our Lord" (Romans 8:38-39). Father Walter returned to the United States after twenty-three years in Siberia marked by years of hardened camp life, yet he was a man deeply in love with God. When he spoke of God or opened the Scriptures, the light of Tabor radiated from his eyes. His life reminds us that the will of God is not a static or imposing force but a dynamic relationship of love that anchors us through the storms of life. To seek the will of God at every moment of every day is to live in the eternal now.

How Do I Know the Will of God?

Many people go through life asking, "how do I know this is the will of God for me?" If you are looking for something like a book or a piece of paper that has written on it "the Will of God for you," you will never find it. The will of God is not an article to be found, and it is not engraved on stone. We cannot know the will of God intellectually; we can only know it through experience, just as we know our spouse or best friend through the experience of love. We know the will of God by doing the will of God, and we do the will of God by living in the love of God.

If the will of God is God's love for us, then we would have to admit that the will of God is not outside us but first and foremost within us. It is the law of God's love planted deep within the human heart. The love of God that has brought us into being contains the very secret of our identity and our reason for being alive. To discover the will of God is to discover the reason for our existence each moment of each day. We do not have to search high and low to find God's love. We have simply to look in a mirror to see who we are, because in who we are God also is. The will of God therefore begins with the love of self, not a selfish or narcissistic self-love, but the love of self as God created me to be, exactly as I am.

The secret of my life lies in God, Thomas Merton wrote. If I find myself I find God, and if I find God then I will find myself. The problem is I cannot find myself, or the self I find is not the self I want to be. I want to be something other than my self, a self I think I need to be so others will find me more attractive or desirable. But the more I strive to be something other than what God created me to be, the further I move away from God and thus from the will of God. God makes things to be themselves, Merton said, and in being oneself lies the glory of God.[6] Just as the wild sunflowers and poppies are saints gazing up into the face of God because they do nothing more than be themselves, so too we must be ourselves to give glory to God.

One of the main causes of division in our consumer culture is the diminishment of the human person through the lure of idols. We are constantly challenged to be something new and different, something other than ourselves. The culture of consumerism is so dominant that many people live with divided selves, in between the true self (which God created) and the false self (which we create), struggling to find their identity.

The further I am from my true self, Merton claimed, the self that God created me to be, the more wrapped up I am in my false self, the self I think I need to be and the one that is farthest from God. Indeed, God knows nothing about this false self because God did not create it. To live in the false self is to lose sight of God because it is a self that God knows nothing about; hence, it is to lose sight of the will of God. Because God knows nothing of this self, the false self is usually restless, distracted, confused, and unhappy. This self, because it is in darkness, demands all my time and attention, turning me away from my true self whose seed of life lies in God.

When we live in the false self, we inevitably choose options in life for the wrong reasons. For example, some people enter into marriage to satisfy their parents, others enter religious life as a way out of debt, while others choose single life to be free of commitments. When we make life choices for reasons that are not oriented toward the fullness of life, the hole of unhappiness in life deepens because the will of God is exchanged for a false self in love with itself and passing things: wealth, fame, recognition, fortune, or pleasure, none of which can bring happiness if they are not first born of the love of God.

However, if I recognize and accept who I am as God created me to be, then I can begin to accept God's love for me—God's will. Only in the true self can I realize that I am here in this place at this time only by the will of God and for no other reason. I may never have existed—or I may have existed in another place at another time. The very fact that I am here is more than mere chance or coincidence. I am here not because I chose to be here as if I could have chosen otherwise. I am here because it is God's will (which is really God's love) that has brought me into being. If I could come to know this love, then I can let go of what I think I should be or where I should be and accept where I am, what I am, and in being who I am, live freely in the glory of God.

The single source of our happiness, therefore, is the love of God that lies within us. Out of this love we have been chosen from all eternity to give glory to God through our individual personalities and our unique creations.

Reflection Questions

- Who is God for me?
- How do I understand the will of God, and how do I seek it?
- How attentive am I to the voice of God in my life and through others whom I encounter?

REFLECTIONS

Second Evening

Prayer

Prayer is about God and our relationship to God. The important questions we ask or the conclusions we draw about prayer center around the "God question," what we say about God or how we understand God's relation to human existence.[7] The God to whom we pray is the God who directs our lives. If the will of God is known best through bonds of love, then the way to nurture relationship with God is through prayer. Prayer is the longing of the human heart for God. It is a yearning and desire for relationship with God, and it is God's attention to our desire: God-in-communion with us. The great spiritual writer Augustine of Hippo captured the longing of the human heart in the beginning of his *Confessions:* "You have made us for yourself O God and our hearts are restless until they rest in You."[8] We long for God because we are created by God, and this longing is both the source of our hope in God and the very thing we resist. Prayer is an awakening to the fact that the fulfillment of my life lies in God.

God delights in creation and loves each of us with a personal love. Prayer, therefore, is God's desire to breathe in me, to be the spirit of my life, to draw me into the fullness of life. When I pray— when I breathe with God—I become part of the intimacy of God's life. The Franciscan theologian, Saint Bonaventure, wrote in his *Soliloquy,* "God is the One who is closer to you than you are to yourself."[9] Prayer is recognizing the intimate in-dwelling of God in our lives, the One who remains faithful in love even when the world around us may fall apart. The author of the Second Letter to Timothy writes that "if we endure, we will also reign with him; / if we deny him, he will also deny us; / if we are faithless, he remains faithful—for he cannot deny himself" (2 Timothy 2:12-13).

Prayer means centering my life in God by "putting aside every care and anxiety," that is, surrendering my heart to God and striving for purity in love. The person who desires friendship with God must strive to be free from all attachments and from all commitments that are exclusively human or in relation to earthly realities. This does not mean that we are to give up our family or friends or sacrifice our desire for a better job or position. Rather, we may understand *attachment* here as possessiveness. We are called to be *dispossessed* of earthly things so as to possess God. To *possess* means to "cling to," to hold on to something so tightly that other possibilities are squeezed out. Parents can possess children or children possess parents; spouses and friends can possess one another. Each of us is called to be spiritually poor, to empty ourselves of all that we cling to so that we may receive the gift of the Holy Spirit who is the giver and gift of life.

To seek the will of God by living in God means to belong to God. Merton claimed that if my mind and heart do not belong to God, then neither do I belong to God. I wander about restlessly in the world wrapped in my false self, unaware that the secret of my happiness lies in the love and mercy of God. Only the pure of heart "see God" because the pure of heart cherish God as the center of their lives. Purity of heart is not simply detachment or self-emptying. Rather it is a total surrender to its only true and most perfect good—union with the Trinity in and through the power of the indwelling Spirit. Our hearts are pure when we view earthly things from "on high," that is, when we see their true value. We "seek the things of heaven" when we search for the mystery of God present in everything, when we realize that all of creation reflects the goodness of God. Since the Spirit of the Lord lives in a pure heart, those who strive for purity of heart are true temples of the Spirit, offering prayer unceasingly to the Father.

To pray is to open up oneself to God who dwells within us. It means holding back nothing from God and sharing everything with God. This opening up to God is God opening up to us. If we are searching for God, it is because God is always searching for us and has already found us. Only the grace of God can enable us to let go of our fears and allow God to be the God of our lives. True prayer is fundamental for life in God. It is that grace of conversion that opens up our hearts to realize the humble presence of God in our lives. Prayer of the heart is unceasing prayer, where God breathes in us and our hearts are turned toward God. This deepening of our lives in the divine life is the path to self-discovery. In and through prayer we discover our true selves, the self that God has created each of us to be. And this self is the Word of God, it is God's self-expression. When we allow our lives to "speak" God, the Word shines forth in our lives. God comes alive in the world.

Life in God should be a daring adventure of love but often we settle for mediocrity. We follow the daily practice of prayer but we are unwilling or, for various reasons, unable to give ourselves totally to God. To settle on the plain of mediocrity is to settle for something less than God, which leaves our hearts restless and unfulfilled. We may seek the will of God as if trying to find a lost coin but we give up too easily. If we desire the will of God, then we must be willing to risk in love. Prayer is that dynamic, life-giving relationship with God by which we grow deep in God's Word, strong in God's grace, and free in God's love to dream with God the unimaginable.

Awakening of the Senses

God is speaking to us all the time, every moment of every day, every season, and every year. God speaks to us through the divine Word that continuously explodes in the universe in thousands of different ways. Merton claimed that every expression of the will of God is in some sense a "word" of God and therefore a "seed" of new life. "The ever-changing reality in the midst of which we live should awaken us to the possibility of an uninterrupted dialogue with God...a dialogue of love and of choice. A dialogue of deep wills."[10] Prayer is attentiveness to the presence of God, awakening to the fact that we are not alone but caught up in God's embrace. It is removing the blinders from our eyes and the rocks from our hearts that isolate and cut us off from knowing God's tender love.

God is speaking all the time because God is love and love desires to express itself. Every event, every situation, every person is an expression of God who is speaking to us. Merton captures this idea beautifully when he writes:

For it is God's love that warms me in the sun and God's love that sends the cold rain. It is God's love that feeds me in the bread I eat and God that feeds me also by hunger and fasting. It is the love of God that sends the winter days when I am cold and sick, and the hot summer when I labor and my clothes are full of sweat: but it is God who breathes on me with light winds off the river and in the breezes out of the woods. His love spreads the shade of the sycamore over my head and sends the water-boy along the edge of the wheat field with a bucket from the spring, while the laborers are resting and the mules stand under the tree....If these seeds would take root in my liberty, and if his will would grow from my freedom, I would become the love that he is, and my harvest would be his glory and my own joy.[11]

If everything around us, within us, and between us is God speaking to us, bending over in love to be close to us, then why do we get lost and wander in darkness? Why is it so difficult for us to find God's will? Perhaps because we are locked up within ourselves, cut off from the sounds, smells, and sights of God's presence. We need an awakening of the senses: eyes to see, ears to hear, hands to touch, a mouth to taste, and a nose to smell the fragrant beauty of God's presence, even in difficult or life-threatening situations. God is love at every moment of every day, through every season, every situation, and every person, but we are blind, deaf, and insensitive to the presence of God. We go about this world as if God is not present or does not exist. We become lost in our thoughts, entangled in our self-concerns, preoccupied with ourselves until one day we find ourselves at a crossroads of decisions and we begin to ask, "what is the will of God?"

In his autobiography *Report to Greco* (Simon & Schuster Adult Publishing Group, publisher), Nikos Kazantzakis tells how a young man went to visit a famous monk in search of the love of God and hope of salvation. He describes their encounter as follows:

Working up courage, I entered the cave and proceeded toward the voice. The ascetic was curled up on the ground. He had raised his head, and I was able in the half-light to make out his face as it gleamed in the depths of unutterable beatitude....

I did not know what to say, where to begin....Finally I gathered up courage.

"Do you still wrestle with the devil, Father Makarios?" I asked him.

"Not any longer, my child. I have grown old now, and he has grown old with me. He doesn't have the strength.....I wrestle with God."

"With God!" I exclaimed in astonishment. "And you hope to win?"

"I hope to lose, my child. My bones remain with me still, and they continue to resist."

"Yours is a hard life, Father. I too want to be saved. Is there no other way?"

"More agreeable?" asked the ascetic, smiling compassionately.

"More human, Father."

"One, only one."

"What is it?"

"Ascent. To climb a series of steps. From the full stomach to hunger, from the slaked throat to thirst, from joy to suffering. God sits at the summit of hunger, thirst, and suffering; the devil sits at the summit of a comfortable life. Choose."

"I am still young. The world is nice. I have time to choose."

Reaching out with the five bones of his hand, the ascetic touched my knee and pushed me.

"Wake up, my child. Wake up before death wakes you up."[12]

Wake up! How many of us are asleep, dreaming of riches and pleasure, when in reality life is happening around us: friends are dying, children are lonely, elderly are abandoned. But we are wrapped up in the layers of our self-concerns, dead to the world of God's people because we are dead to the Spirit of God within us.

To seek the will of God is to wake up to what is alive in us and around us and to what nurtures life for us. Otherwise, death quickly overtakes us and although we seem to be physically alive, we are dragging through life because we are spiritually dead. What does it mean to *be alive?* Is life the biological function of living organisms alone? This is the fundamental question in biomedical ethics today. Can a life-support machine generate life? Many people do not need machines to breathe and yet they are not fully alive, and other people are physically incapacitated and yet fully alive. What distinguishes them? For those who are spiritually dead, each day begins on remote control with the routine of family, work, meals, and sleep. Such people are seldom aware of the needs of the poor, the needs of the natural world, or perhaps even their own spiritual needs because they are spiritually cut off from God and thus from themselves and others. Life continues on automatic pilot until a crisis occurs or one is forced to make a decision. On the other hand, those who are truly alive, even if they are physically impaired, are attuned to the faithful presence of God and delight in the many ways God shows divine love to them, through friends or small deeds of kindness. Life is filled with wonder and beauty, and each day offers itself as a gift to be received and cherished.

To be alive is to be in relationship with God—to have an "other" to whom one can say "thank you." If God is the source of life and indeed life itself, then life means relationship. If we are alive, then we are related to another. One has only to sit in an airport or shopping mall and watch young couples, families with children, or children with elderly parents to realize that life is relational. Each person is related to another person and it is in this relationship that life unfolds. To *be alive* is to participate in the generation of life through relationships and thus to create. Through relationships new ideas are generated, new friendships are formed, new sources of hope are expressed, new beauty is created, new life emerges. If we are locked up within ourselves and experience nothing beyond ourselves—nothing greater than ourselves—then we are probably not alive and certainly not alive to the will of God.

In some ways, the sources of our success today—wealth, degrees, status, material things—are obstacles to our being alive in God. The very things we achieve through hard work force us to become autonomous and self-sufficient, ultimately cut off from others and even from our inner selves. Hence, our achievements can become our difficulties because they may blind us and deafen us to the presence of God. To seek the will of God today, to *be alive,* we must become again like children. Simplicity, purity of heart, and a sense of wonder and awe in the world need rekindling within us: "...unless you change and become like children, you will never enter the kingdom of heaven" (Matthew 18:3-5). Kazantzakis writes: "When I was a child, I became one with sky, insects, sea, wind—whatever I saw or touched....Shutting my eyes contentedly, I used to hold out my palms and wait. God always came—as long as I remained a child."[13] Ronald Rolheiser reminds us that "God will always come to us...as long as we, through the painful purification of our awareness...remain in the perceptive posture of a child."[14] We must undo our wrappings of success if they blind us to the presence of God. We must become vulnerable like children to live freely in the will of God.

Listening: The Art of Obedience

Recently, I was sitting in an airport waiting for my flight that had been delayed because of mechanical trouble. I could not help but overhear the conversation of a young woman sitting next to me, wedded to her cell phone. She was phoning a number of friends, telling them of her weekend visit to a religious community in an effort to explore religious life. At one point I heard her say, "I got along well with all the sisters but I had my eye on the mother superior because I would have to make a vow of obedience and do everything she tells me to do." Of course, I smiled.

When I first entered religious life in January 1984, I sought the most ascetic way of life because I thought this path would lead me most assuredly to God. I joined a community of discalced Carmelite nuns on a small mountain in Pennsylvania and my greatest fear was the vow of obedience. I had been used to living on my own and making independent decisions. How would I handle someone else telling me what (or what not) to do? My fears were realized when one day I was asked to panel a room in a new wing. I protested, saying that I knew nothing about paneling a room. My protests were in vain. That was my assignment, and as one called to obedience, I was to obey the command.

After many years, I have come to appreciate the relationship between obedience and the will of God. Obedience is not a military command or an extrinsic force to control weak human nature. Rather, obedience is relational. The root of *obedience* is the Latin *obodiere*, meaning "to listen." To be obedient is to listen, and listening implies relationship. As one person speaks, so the other listens. Barbara Fiand writes that the traditional view of obedience in religious life led to "conditioned blindness," whereby one blindly obeys a command whether out of fear or for the sake of God. Looking for one's center always outside of oneself, she claims, inculcates a basic sense of unworthiness, distrust of self, and subservience to those "better" or "more qualified" or superior to counsel and guide.[15] Authentic growth demands a movement from an orientation toward heteronomy (finding the law outside) through autonomy (having an inner law) in order to reach an ultimate mature, free relationship with God and the human community in general. Fiand also points out that the obedience of Jesus in the New Testament was more of a "listening in process" than a following of orders.[16] Very few (if any) examples of Jesus indicate he obeyed a command from an authority. His only source of authority was the will of the Father, and his internal relationship (of prayer) with the Father governed his actions.

If seeking the will of God is living in the love of God, then *obedience* is to nurture this love, not suppress it. Obedience is freely giving ourselves over to another out of love. One who lives in obedience must listen attentively. "Listen carefully, my son, to the master's instructions, and attend to them with the ear of your heart," writes Saint Benedict at the beginning of his *Rule*.[17] Listening requires openness, receptivity, a poverty of being insofar as we are ready to receive what we hear into our lives and respond to it. To live in the will of God is to listen to God speaking to us through other people, events in our lives, the beauty of creation, and in the inner heart. But to listen without filters, I must be free of fear, detached from my ideas, without judgment or demands, because if I filter what I hear and impose onto it my own expectations, I may be deaf to the beauty of God's will speaking to me in loving but unexpected ways. Listening to the will of God requires humility, being able to let go of our reigns of control, allowing God to speak to us through weak, fragile humanity even, sometimes, when we do not want to hear what God has to say or find it difficult to accept what we hear.

Solitude

Listening is of the Spirit. It is the spiritual ears of the heart that can discern God's voice in the human voice of another. Francis of Assisi asked his followers to be attentive to the presence of the Spirit in their lives, to have "above all things" the Spirit of the Lord and his holy activity. The Spirit can enter our lives when we make room for God to dwell in our hearts. That is why the perfect Christian prayer is the Our Father. It is a spirit-filled prayer by which we pray, "thy will be done on earth as it is in heaven."

What does this mean, doing God's will on earth as in heaven? It means loving God with our whole heart by making God the center of our lives, with our whole soul by always desiring God, with our whole mind, by directing all our intentions to God and by seeking God's glory in everything. It means loving our neighbor as ourselves by drawing others to God's love and striving to give offense to no one; by rejoicing in the good of others as in our own; and by suffering with others when misfortunes occur. But this is a tall order for a busy world. How can we possibly be so God-filled and God-centered as to devote our entire selves to God? Can we really live in the will of God as a taste of heaven? The answer is *yes*. Not only are we able to live this way, but we are created to live fully in God.

Solitude is essential to finding ourselves in God. Solitude does not mean being alone but being alone with God. To enter into solitude, we need to be still so we can attend to God who comes as a quiet, gentle presence. While this sounds simple, it is really quite difficult for many of us. First, it requires that we take "time out." Slowing down our busy lives in today's world can be dizzying. If and when we stop, we don't know what to do with ourselves. Usually we begin to fill the pockets of time with more things to do: reading, listening to music, walking or some type of sport or exercise. We simply cannot sit quietly for any length of time. Even going on retreat can become busy: sessions to attend, meal schedules, prayer time, and reading time. We cannot be without doing something, and thus we eventually find ourselves in a dilemma of efficient doing and unfulfilled being. We are busy and bored at the same time. Because we never take the time to sit and wait patiently for God, we never find who we really are in God; thus we never become the fullness of person that God has intended us to be.

The only real work in this world is the work of living, of becoming the full human being we are created to be. From our being flows our work—the truer we are to our being, the more effective will be our work because it will be more rooted in God.

Recently, a friend who is a vowed hermit was asked to write of her experience for a local newspaper. She is a talented psychologist and iconographer confined to a wheelchair due to degenerative neuromuscular disease. This is how she described her hermit life:

What is it like they ask
This living in hermitage?
Well, I say...
Nothing is the same.
All of the senses seem centered in the heart.
In solitude the eyes of the heart see,
Nakedly open to reality, but
On a different plane.
I know,
For today I awakened to RAIN.
Praise be to you, sister Spring Rain
You renew the face of the earth
Precious face mirroring the reality
That we are all DRENCHED WITH GOD.
What else can I tell you?
Living in hermitage
Nothing is the same.
All of the senses seem centered in the heart.[18]

What stands out are the capital letters: DRENCHED WITH GOD. We can only become drenched with God if we spend time with God; and here is the key to seeking the will of God.

In a fast-paced, rat-race consumer society, we want things immediately or not at all. Because we have such a variety of things to choose from, if we don't get what we want right away, we simply divert our attention to something else or something we can attain more immediately. Soon we find ourselves multitasking, overstocked, overloaded, and oversized, hopping from one place to another via plane and train, always short on time and indulging ourselves with fast food along the way. We become engulfed in a consumeristic vortex, unable to slow our life's pace to enjoy dinner with a friend or to notice what a poor person looks like as we step around them, scurrying down the sidewalk to who knows where. If we seek to do the will of God, then we must be willing to spend time with God, to begin to see what God looks like and sounds like, as we listen to God in solitude and silence, shutting out the noises and distractions of the world. It is we who must choose God because God has already chosen us.

Obedience is listening to the voice of God's spirit in our lives.[19] Our world is so inundated with noises, the noises of the city, the noises of our cell phones, iPods, the noises of televisions in homes, airports, banks, all the noises of our inner lives. It is difficult for us to hear and especially to hear the voice of God within our hearts. Listening in solitude can be a deafening experience if the forces of inner noise and darkness constantly prevail on us. However, when we can begin to practice the art of patience, slowing down and letting the traffic pass us by, then we begin to appreciate the importance of solitude in our lives. Solitude is necessary if prayer is to be life-sustaining for us in our relationship with God. Without solitude, prayer can be empty words and we become disconnected from the source of life.

Francis of Assisi spent much of his time in solitude. His biographers tell us that he was often confronted by demons and that much of his prayer in solitude was fighting against forces that threatened to separate him from the love of God. One time the devil struggled to drive Francis away from prayer by threatening him with an image of a hunchback woman. His biographer, Thomas of Celano, wrote: "As he began to visit hidden places conducive to prayer, the devil struggled to drive him away with an evil trick. He made Francis think of a horribly hunchbacked woman who lived in town and whose looks scared everyone. The devil threatened that he would become like her if he did not turn back sensibly from what he had begun. But strengthened by the Lord, he rejoiced at a response of healing and grace."[20] The story of the woman indicates that we cannot engage in a life of prayer and solitude without facing the reality of those forces of darkness within ourselves and around us. The woman in Celano's story is a symbol of everything that tries to turn us away from the light of truth. Because we are afraid of holiness, of leaving our selfish selves behind, we do not even try to climb the mountain but pitch our tents in the valley and settle down on the plain of mediocrity.

To be at home with ourselves is to trust God's grace and God's love for us despite the forces of darkness. It is to persevere in prayer, even in the midst of struggle, striving to overcome the obstacles that get in our way of relationship with God. Francis's life was often marked by sadness, disillusionment, and discouragement. His was a contest, a battle, an agony, like Christ himself went through in the Garden of Gethsemane.[21] But Francis trusted God enough not to let go of the divine embrace or to resign from prayer even in the long periods of darkness. His life indicates to us that if we persevere in prayer we will find God in the center of our lives. To trust in the power of God's grace through darkness, isolation, bitterness, and rejection is to be on the way because it is the way to freedom in God. If we can practice solitude each day, we will begin to pray not with words but in a quiet, deep relationship with God who breathes in us. Such practice, however, requires openness to grace and conversion. We must change our unspiritual selves to spiritual selves by allowing ourselves time for solitude, an uncluttered time of stillness where we can begin to hear the movement of the trees and the laughing of rivers. Are we able to stop? Can we hear and what do we hear? Christopher Uhl tells a story that reflects the mutation of our senses. He describes two friends who were walking one day down a busy street in Washington, D.C. One of them was a Native American who worked in the Bureau of Indian Affairs, the other a longtime resident of the city. It was lunchtime and people were rushing down the streets and sidewalks, as car honks and engine noises filled the streets. In the middle of all the traffic, the Indian said, "hey, a cricket!" The other man was amazed. "What?" he said. "Yeah, a cricket," he said again. He pulled aside some bushes that separated the sidewalk from the government buildings. There in the shade was a cricket chirping away. "How did you hear that with all this noise and traffic?" "Oh," said the Native man. "It was the way I was raised...what I was taught to listen for. Here, I'll show you something." The Native man reached into his pocket and pulled out a handful of coins...nickels, quarters, dimes...and dropped then on the sidewalk. Everyone who was rushing by stopped to listen.[22] We with our busy lives, rushing down highways and byways, preoccupied with our own inner thoughts and expectations, what do we hear? What are we listening to?

Reflection Questions

- Does prayer lead me more deeply into the will of God for me? What are some of the signs of God's will in my life?
- Do I encourage solitude for myself and others? Do I fill up my solitude time with things to do, or can I allow myself to face myself in truth?
- If I am married with spouse, children, and a job, do I negotiate for each of us to have "time out," time for solitude or a day of retreat?

REFLECTIONS

REFLECTIONS

Third Evening

Desire

In the Book of Genesis we read that God created humankind in the divine image (see Genesis 1:26). Because we are created in the "image of God" and have the "capacity for God," we are capable of union with God. Today science is revealing parts of the human brain involved with emotion that may also be involved in the experience of God. If the brain is a complex of neural circuits and God cannot be known without the human brain, then we can say we are "wired for God." What these insights suggest, on the most basic level, is that we are biologically oriented toward God. We are truly God-centered human creatures whether or not we want to admit it. If this is true, then we should have no trouble recognizing God's voice when God speaks to us, recognizing God's presence when God appears to us, or recognizing God's embrace when God touches us.

But the fact is, we *do* have trouble recognizing God, however God comes to us. We might say that the tools to know God are all in place; however, they need to be tuned up or fine-tuned or simply acknowledged. God has made it possible to unite with him, but God does not force us into relationship apart from our consent. God is truly mutual in love. Life in God, therefore, is a relationship in love *freely chosen*. If we desire to grow closer to God, we must come to know God, to learn what God is really like, what the voice of God sounds like, and the many ways God can appear to us in this world. Discernment is getting to know God as person, and personally as friend and lover.

As in any relationship, getting to know God is a gradual process.

Discernment presupposes obscurity and ignorance about what God is like or really saying to us. Father Edward Malatesta defines *discernment* as a process by which we honestly confront ourselves and the spiritual movements within us. The purpose of discernment is to decide which movements are of the spirit of God and which are not of God, that is, what brings us closer to God and what separates us from the embrace of divine love.[23]

Although we desire to seek the will of God and desire lures us toward God, unfamiliarity keeps us at a distance. The Holy One we desire we also fear because we are unsure and uncertain of what this closeness might bring. Will my life change? Will I change? Will I lose my friends or make new ones? In human relations, friendship is possible because of a blending of desires. If a person wants to be my friend but I am not attentive to this desire, I may easily overlook his or her efforts to relate to me and thus thwart the desire for friendship. Friendship is possible only when the desires are mutual; they cannot be coerced. Too often relationships become frustrating because of ambivalent or incompatible desires in one or both parties. In a similar way, God's creative touch in our lives is God's desire for us, but we must respond with desire as well. In the Gospels, Jesus asks the blind man, "What do you want? What do you desire?" The blind man responds, "I want to see!" In the same way, God asks us, "What do you want in life?" What is our response? What is our desire?

Discernment is recognizing the voice of God who desires our good. Jesus says to his disciples "the sheep follow him because they know his voice. They will not follow a stranger, but they will run from him because they do not know the voice of strangers" (John 10:4-5). In Palestine, the shepherd would walk ahead of the sheep. Even if the sheep mixed with other sheep at a waterhole, the shepherd could separate his own sheep by just calling them. They knew his voice and they would follow him. To follow the voice of the shepherd is to listen and to trust the one who leads. We might say discernment is choosing the voice we follow. Is it the voice of God or not? How do we know it is the voice of God? What distinguishes it? Is God's voice always sweet and melodious? Can it be angry or sorrowful? Discernment is the art of knowing it is God who is speaking or God who is acting. This art can only be learned by trial and error. It is the process by which we become really "wired for God." Just as we learn the voice of a friend through words of love, support, compassion, and thanksgiving, so too do we learn the voice of God. The voice of a friend is comforting, supportive, and nurturing compared to the voice of the enemy who is hostile, abrasive, threatening, arrogant, or rude. Sometimes we may mistake an enemy for a friend when the words spoken are polite but aggressive and we are led to follow in the direction of that person until an action occurs and we realize that we are being led to the slaughter. Discernment is obedience to the voice of love that God speaks at every moment of our lives. When we find ourselves in perilous situations, it is then we must listen most attentively to the voice of the Holy One within our hearts.

Like Knows Like

Learning to choose God throughout life's journey becomes a way of life for those who practice it. The one who really lives in God learns to grow old with God. As in any relationship, we really get to know another person, such as a friend, spouse, or community member, after many years of living together. We not only recognize their voice or laughter from another room, but we know exactly what to buy for them and what they like to eat. I realized this one Christmas when I went to visit my parents who were married for more than fifty years. My mother wanted to buy my father slippers for Christmas and knew exactly the type she had in mind. We went to several stores and finally I picked out a pair that I thought would be appropriate. She dismissed them quickly with another pair in hand saying, "This is what he likes!" And sure enough he did.

Discernment is striving for clarity of decision when choices are presented or there are many options to choose from. To discern the will of God depends on our lived experience of God. How well do we know God? How open are we to be taught by or to be led by God? The only way to really know God is through the experience of love. That is why prayer is fundamental to discernment. We will never be able to choose the way of God if we are not in some way familiar with God's presence, God's voice, and God's touch.

Just as any relationship requires a rich soil for the fruit of love to grow, so too, discerning God's will requires certain conditions. We already spoke of desire and prayer, but humility and charity are also helpful to discernment. Humility is knowing ourselves with our strengths and weaknesses and allowing others to be themselves as well, without trying to manipulate or control them. A humble person always bends low, so to speak, not lording it over others and ready and willing to learn. Without humility, we can easily overlook the will of God at the present moment, unable to bend low. We are so self-absorbed that we expect everything to come on demand.

Charity, too, is helpful to discernment. The charitable person knows well his or her own weakness and sinfulness and yet is open to the goodness of others. Such a person is slow to judge others, especially if other persons see things differently. The person of charity therefore makes room for personal discernment, recognizing that God's will for one person may be different than for another, even if the person is in the same family or community. When the apostle Peter tried to inquire about Jesus' plans for John, Jesus rebuked him: "If it is my will that he remain until I come, what is that to you? Follow me!" (John 21:22). Discernment, therefore, is keeping our eyes fixed on the Lord and not waiting for others to provide answers to our questions. Even if we seek advice as we struggle to follow Christ, such advice is to help us listen to the breathing of the Spirit in our lives so as to discern God's will.

Although humility and charity are essential for choosing God each day, the wise discerner must also be courageous. If one is truly seeking the will of God and open to the many ways God speaks to us, then one must be courageous and ready to risk. The Danish philosopher Søren Kierkegaard spoke of faith as a "paradox of the absurd" because our "yes" to God is a "yes" to the One who is essentially unknown and beyond rational reason, causing us to step outside our comfortable zones into an abyss of uncertainty. If we are really seeking God, then we must be ready for God—we must accept the grace of God's love. The prophet Isaiah wrote, "For my thoughts are not your thoughts, nor are your ways my ways, says the Lord. For as the heavens are higher than the earth, so are my ways higher than your ways and my thoughts than your thoughts" (55:8-9). If we seek the will of God like a "guaranteed money-back" offer, we will be disappointed. God is mystery and the best that is offered to us is offered in mystery. So we must be able to say "yes" to the hiddenness of God (since hiddenness is the mystery of God). Our "yes" to God is spoken in darkness when we live in faith that God is with us.

But how do we know that the directions of our lives are of God and not some evil spirit? Thomas Green notes the "certitude" concerning God's will for us. He writes, "It is a certitude of faith and not of reason; and it is a practical certitude rather than theoretical."[24] After prayer and reflection one is sure to act in this way here and now, convinced that such action is the only honest, loving thing to do. It may not be the most reasonable thing to do, but if it brings an inner sense of peace and joy, then it is probably the most honest and attuned to the will of God.

Reflection Questions

- Do you pray as one who is "wired for God?"
- In what ways are you attentive to the movements of the Spirit within you?
- What do you desire in the present moment? For your life?

REFLECTIONS

REFLECTIONS

Fourth Evening

Choices

The father of spiritual discernment is Ignatius of Loyola, although the process of discernment can be traced back to the first great theologian of the Church, Origen of Alexandria. In his *Homily XXVII on Numbers,* Origen compares the journey toward God to the passage of the Israelites through the desert into the Promised Land. We begin our journey in life with a desire for happiness and peace but we must pass through the desert, trusting that the God who calls us is with us and will lead us to the promise of life.

Traveling through the desert, however, is difficult because the desert is desolate and filled with the terror of darkness, silence, thirst, and attacks by wild creatures. Origen highlights the value of prayer for discerning good spirits and evil spirits, so that we arrive safely at our destination in God.

While Origen's writings influenced spiritual discernment among the desert fathers and mothers, Ignatius developed the modern process of discernment in his *Spiritual Exercises.* After describing the proper disposition for a good discernment, Ignatius presents to the discerner three occasions when a correct or good choice of a way of life may be made. The *first way* he calls *revelation time.* Here there is no doubt that God is speaking. God's will is so clear that the soul cannot doubt what God wants. Ignatius writes that in a revelation time "God our Lord so moves and attracts the will, that without doubting, or being able to doubt, such devout soul follows what is shown it."[25] We find examples of revelation time in the Scriptures, in the call of Matthew (" 'Follow me.' And he got up and followed him"; Matthew 9:9) and in the story of Saint Paul who was knocked off his horse, blinded, and addressed by Christ himself ("I am Jesus, whom you are persecuting. But get up and enter the city, and you will be told what you are to do"; Acts 9:5–6). A grace-filled moment of revelation is the clearest type of discernment since there is little doubt about God's will; rather, God imprints a certain and firm direction in the heart and there is really nothing one can do to ignore or avoid it.

Decisions in life would be crystal clear if they proceeded on daily revelation alone; however, the way of revelation is the exception and not the norm. The *second way* Ignatius describes is more properly defined as *discernment.* In this way, "light and knowledge," Ignatius says, are "received by experience of consolations and desolations, and by the experience of the discernment of various spirits."[26] This way is a combination of both reason and prayer, patiently waiting for the light of God to direct us and confirm us in our decisions. Ignatius adds that after such a choice or decision, "the person who has made it ought to go with much diligence to prayer before God our Lord and offer Him such election, that His Divine Majesty may be pleased to receive and confirm it, if it is to His greater service and praise."[27] Ignatius' second way can be seen between his first and third ways, the first way being a time of clear revelation and third way a time of great uncertainty concerning God's will. The two are similar in that in both cases there is nothing to discern. But as Thomas Green points out, "this 'nothing' of the third way is a frustrating nothing; that is, in contrast with the clarity and certainty of the revelation time, here God does not seem to be saying anything to the soul sincerely seeking his will."[28] Ignatius states that this third way is a time of peacefulness "when the soul is not acted on by various spirits, and uses its natural powers freely and tranquilly."[29] The use of the word *tranquility* here does not mean peace but the ability to use one's natural powers of reasoning and imagination to weigh the pros and cons of the situation and come to a reasonable decision concerning God's will. One might see here God's respect of the human intellect and freedom to choose. We are not only asked to pray for light and courage but we are asked to use our intellect to weigh the matters before us with care and fidelity. Ignatius tells us that after we have considered every side of the matter, then we need to weigh the alternatives. Which choice seems reasonable and gives me peace of mind and heart? What are the reasons for my decision? Are they selfish reasons, or do they flow from deep prayer and honesty with God? [30]

Although Ignatius emphasizes human reason in the second way, he also asks us to use our imagination. How would I advise another person facing the same choice? Would I make this choice on my deathbed? Can I live with this choice as I face God on the last day or the final judgment? [31] Sometimes decisions become clear as we weigh the pros and cons or try to advise someone else in a similar situation. How often have we given advice to others and upon hearing it said, "How strange! I have said that to others. Why could I not see it as relevant to myself?" "The reason," Green states, "is that we find it difficult to distance ourselves from our own problems and to look at them 'objectively.'" [32] That is why when we live in spiritual poverty and humility, in spiritual openness, we can see ourselves reflected better in others than in ourselves, for the other is a reflection of ourselves. The other is a mirror of God.

Although Ignatius emphasizes the use of the intellect and reason in discerning the will of God, it also is important to highlight the role of the heart. The Franciscan theologian, Saint Bonaventure, describes the affective capacity of the human person, that is, the human person's potential to be moved by desire for the good. He writes that "human desire is directed at nothing but the supreme Good, or that which leads to it or reflects the Good in a certain way."[33] Since desire is born in the human heart, Bonaventure urges the spiritual pilgrim to "enter into one's innermost self and make good use of one's cognitive and affective powers in the struggle for wisdom."[34] To "enter into the heart" is to be attentive to one's inner feelings and movements and to confront these feelings and movements honestly. One might speak of "obedience to the heart" as listening attentively to the small voices that speak within us and direct us to what is closest to the highest Good.

In his instruction *On the Perfection of Life*, Bonaventure tells us that if we are to arrive at true self-knowledge (and thus knowledge of God), then we must enter into our heart; that is, we must stop the busyness and frantic activity of our lives and return to ourselves. According to Bonaventure, we are to have a conversation with ourselves, discussing what we are at present, what we were, and what we can be if we acknowledge our faults and failings. Then he says we must consider what we can be if we stop trying to control our lives and open up to the grace of God.[35]

Bonaventure assures his readers that whoever persists in searching the heart will find there a precious treasure, for "where your treasure is, there your heart will be also" (Matthew 6:21; Luke 12:24). Perhaps one of the most difficult challenges today is confronting our own hearts; we fear what we may find there. Yet the more we ignore what is in our hearts, the greater we experience darkness and confusion. For the heart is the dwelling place of God; it is in the heart that God humbly waits for us to respond in love. To listen to the heart and to be attentive to its movements toward the highest good is to seek the will of God.

In his book *Swimming in the Sun*, Albert Haase describes five factors that must be considered if we are to maintain a balance between head and heart. He describes these as follows:

- *My past history*—My upbringing,
  the values I have assimilated, my family life and my past.
- *My potential*—my talents and abilities.
- *My present identity*—my self-knowledge and my
  commitment to others, either as married,
  single or religious.
- *My hopes, dreams and desires*—
  what do I imagine and hope for?
- *My free heart*—what option or decision makes
  me happy?[36]

The key to freedom of heart is the ability to accept oneself without the need to try to be someone else, to please others, or to live up to false expectations. Only when the heart is free can one then choose a path in life, trusting that the goodness of God will enlighten this journey. One of best examples of this type of freedom is found in Francis of Assisi's "Letter to Brother Leo" where he says to Leo, "I speak to you, my son, as a mother....If it is necessary for you to come to me for counsel, I say this to you: In whatever way it seems best to you to please the Lord God and to follow his footprints and his poverty, do this with the blessing of God and my obedience."[37] Francis indicates that Leo must have self-knowledge and brutal honesty if he is a man committed to the dream of Gospel life. Haase writes, "From the Franciscan perspective, true obedience to the will of God, in imitation of Christ, is a positive expression of a person's freedom and creativity."[38] That is, if we really desire to live in harmony with God's will, then we must discover our own unique way of contributing to Jesus' kingdom of peace, justice, and love. We must graciously accept that fact that we are loved by God into being.

Consolation

Although we may not "hear" God speaking to us most of the time and are unsure whether or not we are really following God, there are signs of God's intimate presence with us. However, we first have to realize that God does not shout or scream. God does not make loud sounds or dramatic changes to show his presence. Rather, God speaks most eloquently in stillness and silence. The sixth-century mystical writer, Pseudo-Dionysius, said that God speaks most clearly in silence. In fact, the more language we need to talk about God, the further away we are from God. The closer we come to God, the fewer words we need to speak of God, as when two people who have known each other for such a long time that presence, not conversation, is usually the language between them. God is closer to each of us than we are to ourselves, Bonaventure once wrote. The mystery of God is so profound and incomprehensible that words fail to describe God. The closer God is to us, the less we can really describe this divine presence in words that convey the depth of the experience of God.

So how do we know we are in right relationship with God? How do we know we are living the will of God? Ignatius tells us that we know by the movements within the soul that indicate the nearness of God. In the third rule of his *Spiritual Exercises,* Ignatius says that we can identify the right path when we experience consolation within us that is usually marked by a greater love of God or a feeling of peace or joy. We know this feeling not as an ordinary feeling but one that can surprise us by its depth and power. But we can also experience consolation when one sheds tears out of love of God because of sorrow for sins, because of the sufferings of Christ our Lord, or for any other reason that is immediately directed to the praise and service of God. However we experience consolation—

either through deep peace or tears—such consolation increases one's faith, hope, and love and acts as an invitation to love, praise, and glorify God. Consolation is the grace of God welling up within us, filling us with an ineffable heart of love. Our only true response can be a greater act of love.[39]

How do we know God is present to us and we are in right relationship with God? Ignatius relies on human experience: an increased love of God; compunction or a sense of sorrow for one's sins; an increase of faith and hope, joy, peace; and quiet deep within the soul or the deepest center of one's being. Thomas Green states more succinctly that the common denominator for discerning the will of God is *peace* in the Lord: "whether the soul be deeply or strongly moved, as in the emotional reunion of two lovers after a long separation, or quietly consoled, as might be the experience of a mother gazing on. . .her newborn child. . .and quietly marveling at the wonder of life which has come from her body."[40] Our emotions cannot form our complete litmus test with God, as many factors influence our emotional life; nonetheless, they are essential to the spiritual life and to discerning God's will for us. As in any relationship, feelings are crucial and this is no less true for a relationship with God. Feelings or emotions are our "raw data" on which we reflect as we evaluate them with our intellect to discern the will of God. The intellect helps us sort through the complexity of our emotions so that when the forces of life become like gale storms, we still sense deep within us a certain peace that signifies the will of God. Thus, we know we are living in the will of God when at the end of a day we can pray with a deep sense of gratitude and peace: "For all that has been, thanks. For all that will be, yes!"[41]

Desolation

If peace is the mark of God's consoling presence, then it is reasonable that a feeling of abandonment by God or the sense that traveling the wrong path shows itself in lack of peace. Desolation reveals itself in deep inner anxiety where, despite the best efforts of friends or family members to provide consolation, peace or joy cannot be found. Saint Ignatius describes the period of desolation as a time of darkness in the soul, turmoil of spirit, listlessness, ambivalence, indecisiveness, and restlessness that can lead to lack of faith, hope and love. A basic sadness subsists within the soul that renders it lost and separated from its Creator and Lord. Just as consolation brings inner peace, desolation results in lack of peace, confusion, and darkness.[42]

The period of desolation is difficult to persevere through because this period of darkness is sometimes accompanied by feeling of abandonment, emptiness, or failure. The heart experiences a conflict of movements, and the desire for the highest good is obscured by darkness, silence, or the inability to choose what is the highest good. When I was in graduate school at Fordham University, I lived next door to a young woman whose husband had just left her. She told me that they had been married for ten years and had, what she thought, was a happy marriage. One day, however, he came home and announced that he no longer wanted to be married, simply because he wanted to be single again. She was devastated and for months tried to figure out what she had done wrong. She stopped eating and became insomniac and eventually turned to prayer for some type of comfort. She went through a long period of desolation and blamed herself for the divorce. During this time she sought spiritual advice and became involved with a Third Order group of Carmelites, eventually becoming professed as a Third Order Carmelite. Through her studies at Fordham and her involvement with the Carmelites, she began to regain her life and eventually became a spiritual director.

Although desolation is not a state we usually desire, it can serve a positive function in our lives by alerting us to the need for change or for new decisions. Desolation, therefore, like consolation is a period of grace and, we might say, the presence of God's hidden light. The light of God is within us but we cannot see it because, for various reasons, we have made choices that obscure God's presence in our lives.

Beginners in the spiritual life are often vulnerable to desolation because they try to control their spiritual lives rather than entrusting them to God. When self-will prevails over God's will, we may leave the front door of our hearts open for evil spirits to enter, bringing with them discouragement, anxiety, restlessness, fear, and loss of peace. The great Italian saint, Catherine of Bologna, spent many years in darkness and depression, embattled by evil spirits and diabolical temptations. Over time, she learned to trust God completely, despite the darkness, realizing that trust and hope in God will give us his grace by which we will have complete victory over our enemies. God does not abandon those who hope in him.

God is always faithful to us but we must choose God, even in times of desolation. If we choose to remain in desolation indefinitely, as if a lack of peace and joy may be God's will for us, we will miss out on life and on the opportunity to love God in new ways.

God does not desire our unhappiness nor does God dwell where there is no peace. Rather, God desires the fullness of life for us. Thus, Ignatius advises "[i]n time of desolation never to make a change; but to be firm and constant in the resolutions and determination in which one was the day preceding such desolation, or in the determination in which he was in the preceding consolation."[43] The reason for this, Ignatius states, is that just "as in consolation it is rather the good spirit who guides and counsels us, so in desolation it is the bad, with whose counsels we cannot take a course to decide rightly."[44] Although Ignatius links desolation and evil spirits, I do not think that desolation is necessarily a time of evil. Jesus himself was led to the desolation of Gethsemane, not by an evil spirit but by the love of God. Here he experienced his final test of faith, tried like gold in a fire, so that only the purity of his intention to love remained. Desolation can be a time of growth when we trust God by letting go of our fears, expectations, or sense of failure and allowing God's grace to enter in. The depth of our love may be tested in the desolation of the desert so that we may truly belong to God.

Reflection Questions

- When have you felt a glimmer of God's presence? How did you know?
- What criteria do I use to make decisions in my life?
- Do I make decisions out of a free heart or one that is heavy with cares and anxieties?
- How do I recognize desolation in my life? How have I coped with it? Do I try to escape it, or do I see it as graced time?

REFLECTIONS

REFLECTIONS

Fifth Evening

Sifting Out
God's Love

If growing in the love of God or attuning ourselves to God's will is a movement between consolation and desolation, it is because life swings between moments of change and decisions. Life is an ebb and flow of relationships between persons and between creatures and God. While consolations provide comfort and support, life in God is not a lifetime guarantee of warm, cozy feelings.

The life of Jesus Christ signifies to us that the path to God is narrow and often winding and dangerous. "If any want to become my followers," Jesus said, "let them deny themselves and take up their cross daily and follow me" (Luke 9:23). Life in God is risky; death is involved and trust is needed. How do we come to live in the presence of God, that is, in God's will, with the cross at the center of our lives? We come to live in God's will through faith in God's incomprehensible love for us, hope in things unseen, and love as the desire to live in the good. Each day must be a choice for God anew.

The saints are often models of what life in God is like, as we seek to grow in the abundance of God's love amid the weeds or evil spirits of the world. We do not have to look too far back in time to find women and men of outstanding holiness who persevered in love despite persecution, darkness. and the threat of death. We have already mentioned the life of Father Walter Ciszek (1904-1984), who survived twenty-three years of imprisonment in Russia. We find another example of holiness in the life of Father Arseny (1893-1973), an Orthodox priest who survived the hardships of a concentration camp and emerged as a beacon of light. Like Father Walter, Father Arseny lived the will of God amid the brutality of a Soviet prison camp. By focusing his life on God and the following of Christ, he lived by the injunction to "bear one another's burdens, and in this way...fulfill the law of Christ" (Galatians 6:2). With a spirit of genuine charity and compassion he comforted the afflicted, reconciled enemies, protected the poor, and fed the hungry. His tremendous love of every human being, including the most hardened of criminals, led to conversions in the concentration camp, including the confession of religion among declared atheists. One of the most (of many) inspiring stories of his life was his mediation between a young man who had recently been sent to the camp and some criminals who had tried to rob him. Father Arseny interceded on behalf of the young man and as a result the young man and Father Arseny were punished by solitary lockup in a frozen Siberian shed, with no heat, for several days. According to the story, Father Arseny prayed day and night and he and the young man experienced a warmth in the frozen shed, thus never succumbing to death.

Thankfully, confinement in a concentration camp is not a prerequisite for growth into holiness. Years ago I remember reading a story about a mother and wife who did extraordinary acts of love in the most ordinary way, never realizing the positive impact of her life on those around her. She was a deeply spiritual woman, committed to daily Mass and prayer, even though she was responsible for the care of her children and her elderly mother. The story described her heroic deeds of going out in the middle of a snowstorm to help an elderly neighbor, of staying by her husband's side when he lost his job after twenty-five years, and best of all driving a hundred and fifty miles each week to care for an elderly man whose wife had been her hairdresser for many years and had died. The story emphasized that holiness unfolds in everyday life when God is the center of life.

To choose God each day is to grow as wheat among the weeds of the world. It is to persevere in love, despite the forces that prevail against us. In the Gospel of Matthew, Jesus tells us that life is a mixture of weeds and wheat:

> *The kingdom of heaven may be compared to someone who sowed good seed in his field; but while everybody was asleep, an enemy came and sowed weeds among the wheat, and then went away. So when the plants came up and bore grain, then the weeds appeared as well. And the slaves of the householder came and said to him, "Master, did you not sow good seed in your field? Where, then, did these weeds come from?" He answered, "An enemy has done this." The slaves said to him, "Then do you want us to go and gather them?" But he replied, "No; for in gathering the weeds you would uproot the wheat along with them. Let both of them grow together until the harvest; and at harvest time I will tell the reapers, Collect the weeds first and bind them in bundles to be burned, but gather the wheat into my barn"* (Matthew 13:24–30).

While the wheat and weeds may refer to types of people in the world, they may also refer to the fields of our own inner lives, as Thomas Green suggests. We desire the good but we may find ourselves choosing other than the good. "The wheat of our virtues—trust, humility, gratitude, zeal—could not come to full maturity," Green states, "without the weeds of our instinctual failings."[45] Our goodness and desire for holiness is mixed with selfish love until we can learn to purify our hearts of self-centeredness, release our need for control, and allow ourselves to be completely dependent on God.

The pure of heart look down on the things of earth while seeking the things of heaven, Francis of Assisi proclaimed.[46] We do not have to be in a monastery to attain purity of heart, but we do need to be in the cave of our heart to seek God. It is from here we can begin to see the world with the eyes of love.

Discernment: A Spiral of Love

The saints indicate to us that living in God's love is living with continuous desire. Desire is the gravity of our lives, born out of the deepest spiritual center within us; therefore, to be attuned to our desires is to be attuned to the direction of our lives. Thomas Merton once wrote, "Life is shaped by the end you live for. You are made in the image of what you desire."[47] The problem with desire in today's world is twofold: Desires tend to be superficial and demand immediate satisfaction. Most of us do not know our deepest desires or mistake unfulfilled wants for deeper longings. Unfulfilled wants lead to unbridled wants, and we find ourselves yearning after things we don't really want or need. What we fail to realize in our consumer culture is that desire is not meant to be controlled by fulfillment; rather, desire is the most honest indicator of what our lives are about. Desire is born of the Spirit and thus is God's gift to us, luring us into the fullness of life. Desire is not born of need but of grace. That is why desire is the pulse of our lives because it is the pulse of our hearts. Desire directs our lives in their deepest longings. If our desires are misguided, so too, will the choices of our lives be misguided. Desire requires honest, attentive listening to our inner hearts where we discover what we hope for and what will transform our lives.

Desire awakens us every morning of a new day. Choosing God is a daily act of desire when our hearts are directed toward God; each moment of our lives must be a choice for God. It may seem unreasonable to choose God at every moment when our lives are filled with many things: things to think about, things to do. How do we attain "God-centeredness" instead of "self-centeredness"? The saints who are the holy ones of God indicate to us that the only way to "God-centeredness" is through practice. We must learn to "practice God." This is another way of saying that we need a "God-consciousness," which comes about through prayer, breathing in God, and a mindfulness of God, which expresses itself in love. Spirituality is a transformation of consciousness from self-consciousness toward God-consciousness, that is, toward a divine Other to whom we belong and in whom we find our fulfillment. We might describe the spiritual life as refocusing our ego toward God—the "I" of the self is no longer centered in the self but in God. When we "practice God" daily we live discerning lives; we live with an inner peace or consolation, knowing that times of desolation are times of trial or signals to orient ourselves to God in a new direction. Discernment becomes integral to the daily practice of loving like God when we begin to harvest the wheat of our lives even though weeds may still grow within us. God becomes part and parcel of our lives, and desire keeps us yearning for ever-greater closeness to the One who is intimately near to us.

The fourth-century writer Gregory of Nyssa described a movement of perpetual growth of the soul *(epektasis)* that helps us understand discernment as constant choice for life in God. *Epektasis* expresses the soul's constant motion forward as it forgets what is past and continually opens to new graces. The soul is conceived as a spiritual universe in eternal expansion toward the infinite source of love. On one hand is a certain contact with God, a real participation and divinization. But God who is *infinite* love remains constantly beyond, and the soul must always go out of itself; it must continually go beyond the stage it has reached to make a further discovery. Thus each individual stage is a "glory," but the brilliance of each stage is always being obscured by the new "glory"—the soul moves from glory to glory (see 2 Corinthians 3:18). For Gregory, the soul's security is in change. Change is the mark of spiritual growth, whereas sin is the ultimate refusal to grow. Each new stage of spiritual growth is the development of a reality that is entirely new. The journey into God is like a spiral. Every stage of growth in the soul is an absolute beginning or, we might say, every end is a beginning, and every arrival is a new departure. In this way, discernment is not something we do at stages of our lives or at the crossroads of life's changes. Rather, discernment is the way we *live in* God, in the dynamic movement of the soul's deepest desire. When life presents a series of choices, the compass of our lives should always be pointing in the same direction—toward God—so that whatever concrete decision we make will ultimately have God at its center.

Reflection Questions

- What are the weeds and the wheat in my life?
- Do I practice discernment as a way of living in God?
- Am I patient with myself as I seek to live in God's love?
- In which direction is my life pointed: weeds or wheat?

REFLECTIONS

REFLECTIONS

Sixth Evening

The Gravity of Love

The author of the fourth Gospel in a short letter to his disciples wrote that "God is love" (1 John 4:8). To say God is love means that love defines God. Love is what God is. God is not something other than love; rather, God *is* love. As a child, I pictured God as an elderly grandfather who rewarded good children and punished wicked ones. I imagined that God's love was like going for an ice cream sundae in the middle of Lent—an awesome experience.

It has taken me many years to plumb the revelation—God *is* love—personal, relational, transforming, and unitive love. If we take a moment to ponder the love that God is, we have a glimpse of the divine life. The fountain fullness of love, the Father, who is without beginning, infinite and incomprehensible in love, overflows in love to another who is not the Father but fully expresses the Father: the Word of the Father, who is the Son. The Son is everything the Father is in one other than the Father. The love between the Father and Son is eternal, dynamic, and mutual love, and they breathe love for one another in a spiritual bond that is expressed in the person of the Spirit. If we ask, "What is God?" we would have to answer, "God is a communion of persons in love."

We humans and all creation are created through the Father's loving expression in the Word/Son and thus we are created within this communion of love. Because we are created through the Word, we are finite expressions of the infinite love of God. Just as the Father's love overflows into the Son, so too God's love overflows into us, and just as the Son yearns for the Father, so too we yearn for God. In Psalm 42 the author speaks eloquently of the heart's yearning for the beloved: "My soul thirsts for God, / for the living God. / When shall I come and behold / the face of God?" (Psalm 42:2). The Spirit of love who is the bond between the Father and Son is the same Spirit who breathes within us the desire and yearning for God.

When will we arrive and behold God's face? According to Gregory of Nyssa, the answer is never or, we might say, the closer we come to see God's face, the more it eludes us. Life in God is always a yearning after the One who is incomprehensible love. This may sound like an exhausting search but it means the closer we come to God, the more we will desire God. It is not distance but nearness that enkindles our heart for the beloved. To grow near to God is to spend time with God. If we give minimum time to God we might expect minimum love in return—a lukewarm if not confused heart. Just as we are what we eat, undoubtedly we also are what or who we love. If we find ourselves divided among many loves we wind up loving no one or nothing, including ourselves. We may have many loves, but we cannot be divided among many loves. Surrender is making a choice for love. It is not asking "How will this love benefit me?" Rather, it affirms that love is stronger than death. We should never fear the gravity of God's love, for "perfect love casts out fear" (1 John 4:18). We are created to transcend ourselves in love, not to be satiated in it or perhaps bored by it. God's love is ecstatic, according to Pseudo-Dionysius, and we can become drunk on love, inebriated with it, if we allow ourselves to be drawn out of ourselves in love.[48]

Trust

If we desire the will of God and yearn for God, we can be sure that risk and challenge will accompany us on the journey. Many spiritual writers from Saint Paul to Augustine, to Thomas Merton in our own time, speak of human life caught between two wills: self-will and the will of God. The former pulls us away from God and the latter toward God. Usually, we favor one direction or another, but sometimes we are caught in between, as Paul wrote in his Letter to the Romans: "So I find it to be a law that when I want to do what is good, evil lies close at hand. For I delight in the law of God in my inmost self, but I see in my members another law at war with the law of my mind, making me captive to the law of sin that dwells in my members" (7:21-22). How can we be caught between two wills if we are really embraced in the communion of God's love? Are we caught up in the love of the Trinity or not? The answer is *yes, we are.* However, God loves us freely and we are to respond freely in love—without ulterior motives or by coercion or for any other reason than loving God for God.

God bends low in love, Saint Bonaventure wrote. Yet we humans in our sinful nature are turned away from God, blinded in intellect, distorted in our desires, and entangled in endless questions. "The human person is endlessly asking and begging," Bonaventure said. "Covetousness is never satisfied."[49] So while God bends over in love for us, we are bent over in love for ourselves, caught in a web of self-centeredness to the extent that we fail to grasp the hand of God; we fail to see the humility of God. To live in relation to a humble God we must stand upright in order to know truth, to love rightly, and to act justly. "This occurs," Bonaventure says, "when someone turns completely away from self and toward God."[50] While the grace of God helps us turn in the right direction, God's grace is marked by freedom. God will not force our love; rather, we must say "yes" to God, a "yes" that is free.

Human freedom is grounded in divine freedom. Perfect love is perfectly free. The Fathers of the Church recognized that God becomes *powerless* before human freedom; he cannot violate it since it flows from his own omnipotence. Simply put, God creates human freedom; therefore, God cannot violate what he creates. Although we are created out of God's love, God's will, we cannot be saved by the will of God alone. Rather, God needs our cooperation, our consent to be like God. God does not impose divine love on us, forcing us to love God; rather, God's love is so profound and humble that it bends low in weakness and suffering to be where we are so that we may be where God is. As the Orthodox theologian Vladimir Lossky wrote, "the *Divine will* always submits itself to detours, even to revolts of *human will* to bring it to a free consent...God [is] a beggar of love waiting at the soul's door without ever daring to force it"[51] [emphasis added]. If God waits patiently for us to answer the call to love, how could we ever imagine God to be a tyrant or a vengeful God unless we project onto God our own fears of human power?

God begs at the door of our souls, but it is only we who can open the door and invite God in. Just as we do not readily invite strangers into our home, neither do we invite God in if God is a stranger to us. Faith in God is not enough; we must also trust this God of love who invites us into the divine life, to share this life. How often in the Scriptures Jesus says to his disciples to have faith and trust. To accept another without conditions, without proof, without bartering is to trust the One who is a beggar of love and who begs for our love. To do the will of God is to invite the beggar of love into the home of our inner hearts. To trust this beggar of love is to give everything we have and everything we are over to him. It is to surrender.

Surrender: Giving Up or Giving Over?

Recently I attended a retreat and at the end of the retreat the director asked each person to take a penny from a bowl and ponder the words "In God We trust." It is ironic these days to ponder trust in God on a coin, for money has become the god of many people. Money is power and power is control. Where there is control and power there is no need to trust, only to possess. Power and possession can force a type of surrender. In the case of war, the one who takes possession of a land and its people can force the captured opponent or enemy to surrender. This type of surrender is one of defeat, of losing the battle, forcing the one who is captured to hand over one's weapons. A surrender of defeatism can also show itself in the person in whom a terminal illness is diagnosed and who no longer desires to live. The will to live is conquered by the illness, in the same way that someone captured in war is conquered by the enemy. In either case, surrender means giving up the will to live or fight because one is overpowered by something much larger than oneself.

Surrender to God, however, is not giving up in the face of overwhelming power; it is not a defeat of the will's desires. Rather, it is giving oneself over freely to God. It is recognizing that the power of God does not overwhelm or conquer; rather, it is recognizing that God's love empowers us for life. We have a difficult time trusting in the power of God's unconditional love because we want a visible, tangible power or we want to control divine power ourselves. To surrender in any situation usually means giving up self-power and control. Yet, God's love, through our full surrender to it, empowers us.

Can one surrender and not give oneself away? Yes, if one is conquered by a force larger than oneself and against one's will or desire. But the type of surrender that immerses one in the will of God is a freely chosen self-surrender. It is a letting go into God that empowers us to go forth freely in life. That is, surrender to God empowers us to live freely, secure in the embrace of God's love, knowing that our lives come from God and belong to God.

Surrender expresses the poverty of being human, which means radical dependency on God. The truly poor person hangs on to the threads of God's gracious love. He or she recognizes that life is radically contingent; nothing has to be the way it is. Everything is gift.

In an article on "The Sacrament of Creation," Michael and Kenneth Himes describe poverty—not economic poverty but poverty of being—as the definition of life. They write, "The discovery of one's finiteness is the recognition of one's poverty. When one grasps the 'iffiness' of one's existence, the shocking fact that the source and foundation of one's being is not in oneself, then one knows oneself as truly poor."[52] Everything is gift. Poverty impels us to reflect on our lives in the world from the position of weakness, dependency, and vulnerability. It impels us to empty our pockets—not of money—but the pockets of our hearts, minds, wills—those places where we store up things for ourselves and isolate ourselves from real relationship with others. Poverty calls us to be vulnerable, open, and receptive to others, to allow others into our lives and to be free enough to enter into the lives of others. Only when we can let go of what we cling to and let God be the God of our lives do we begin to live in the will of God.

Surrender to God is the beginning of heaven because only when we place our entire trust in God can God's love take hold of us and transform us into what we are created to be: the face of God's compassionate love. When we allow God to take up residence in every atom of our being, in every moment of our existence, in every place of our life, then we live in the grace of surrender. David Brenner writes that surrender to God means giving ourselves over completely to God, "open to receiving the trust that God will give us so that our life may be a *yes* to the initiatives of divine love."[53] Surrender, therefore, is a grace-filled choice to rely wholly on God. It is the poverty of letting go and letting be, trusting in God's ever-faithful love. God's desire is for us to be *God with us.* This is the meaning of Jesus Christ. But what do we want? What do we desire?

Reflection Questions

- Do I trust God enough to let go and allow the movements of life to unfold beyond my immediate power to control?
- Can I freely give myself to God in love?
- What prevents me from living as a poor person, that is, dependent on the love and mercy of God?

REFLECTIONS

Seventh Evening

Love's Sweet Surrender

Surrender to God presupposes a relationship with God rooted in love, trust, and hope in God's personal desire for us. It is the art of yielding to another despite the forceful will of the self that seeks survival and protection. Surrender expresses one's belief that God is love and love never fails. We would be remiss to think, however, that surrender is a movement in trust and love only on our part, as if God might be waiting for us to hand over the reins of control. Such an idea misses out on the tremendous mystery of God as love, for our surrender to God is based on God's surrender *to us*.

In the Incarnation, God gives Godself to us, completely and unconditionally, unto death. We could not give ourselves wholly to God if God had not first given Godself to us. Revelation is the descent of God into our poor, frail human condition. God surrenders God's self to us in love. Through divine surrender God reveals the riches of divine love. The surrender of God in the person of Jesus Christ is the great mystery of God. God does not hold back and wait until we get things right; rather, God loves us where we are and as we are. In the Incarnation, divine love has found us and has surrendered to us. It has handed itself over to us to do as we please.

What do we do with this tremendous gift of divine love so freely given to us? Some of us are blind to this love, so we ignore it. Others do not believe that God surrenders—completely in love with us—and therefore reject it. Still others fear that a God of self-giving love could be weak, and so they question the divine love. But for those who breathe in the Spirit of God, the surrender of God in love is the greatest act of humility, and one can only receive this love in poverty and humility. Receptivity marks the person of surrender.

Francis of Assisi knew that the human person has a tendency to cling and to possess because possession is integral to humanity's sinful condition. We possess not only material things; we also possess attitudes, behaviors, and feelings. We control our lives and thus we control how much we are willing to give over (surrender) to God (and thus to our neighbors). According to Francis, such a person cannot surrender freely to God because he or she is neither poor nor humble. Rather the poor person—the one who lives in surrender to God's love—is the one who has space within his or her heart to receive God. The one who has made space within for God to dwell is the one who can surrender to God. Indeed, without this inner space for God's indwelling we miss out on the entire drama of God's incarnate love.

God's love surrenders itself in the most ordinary way, in weak, fragile human beings and in the fragile things of creation. But without spiritual eyes and a heart centered in God we could easily mistake God in daily life for a stranger, an alien, or simply a "nobody," one who is not important to us. Francis believed that the humility of God is apparent only to those who are living in "penance" or conversion, those who are striving to turn their hearts toward God and live in God. Such persons see with spiritual eyes. To see with the eyes of the heart is to live in surrender to God.

Holding On:
Control and Power

The problem with surrendering to God or accepting God's surrender to us lies in the selfish gene for control and power. We live in an age of control and power. By *control* we mean the ability to govern our lives, make independent decisions, and act as independent agents—to be our own "gods," so to speak. Worldly power expresses itself in control; usually the greater the power we have, the greater control. No matter how much we desire global justice and unity in the world, power and control mark contemporary human life, especially in the First World, which holds the majority of the world's wealth.

Recently I spent a week at a retreat house on the New Jersey shore. Every day I took a walk and admired the beautiful homes nestled together like little villages on the English coast. I was struck by the size of the homes and the variety of architectural designs until I realized one day that almost all the homes had their blinds drawn. No one was living in them. I was told that they were second and third homes, vacation homes that would soon come to life with the summer season. Since I have never owned a home, I wondered why people accumulated large homes and furnished them elaborately, only to live in them for several weeks a year. The only reason I could find was control and power, not control over others but control over one's private life, control of security, comfort, protection, freedom, autonomy, and space. The desire for control and power can spill over easily to affect our life in God. If our relationship with God is limited by control, how much time will we give to God, and how might we expect God to secure our lives in the world?

The problem with control and power is illusion. We think we own and possess things; we act as if we are more powerful than the next person but without surrender to God, everything we have and possess may be taken from us in a blink of an eye. Unbridled control and power blind us to the truth of our lives in God. North American society is witnessing the age of "McMansion," building heaven on earth according to personal desires and accumulated wealth. The only things we truly possess, according to Francis of Assisi, are our vices and sins.[54] The rest are all gifts, loaned to us on borrowed time.

Some people never learn this truth because they die young. Others learn it through the difficult path of aging and diminishment. Only death can teach us the meaning of life's riches because in the end we stand naked before God. The only way to overcome the disease of control and power is surrender.

Not too long ago a close family friend took his life by suicide. He seem to have "had it all"—good looks, money, friends, material comforts, a good job, and a supportive, loving family. He was always very affable in social circles. We learned afterward that his immediate family knew of his depression but kept it secret. They tried to control the situation and, in some ways, tried to control his life. Although they had his best interests in mind, control and power led to destruction.

Surrender is most difficult perhaps when the situation involves someone we love and the one we love is hurting or in pain. Yet, this is what surrender means—not to control another person's life or even our own lives but to face life in truth, to accept the fragility of our lives, and to allow God to help heal our wounds through the stranger or the one outside our immediate control. To surrender is to hand ourselves over to another in love. Surrender means radical trust in God and in the human person who is the image of God.

We can spiritualize surrender by praying words of surrender but fail to change our attitude or behaviors, holding on and controlling our relationship with God and others. Living as masters of control and power prevents us from being truly human because we cut ourselves off from others; we choose to remain isolated rather than related. People become obstacles to our otherwise private lives. To be a human person is to be in relationship, open to others and receiving from them. The poor person, the one who lives dependent on God, can teach us about surrender because he or she lives in openness and gratitude for all of life's gifts. When we live in the grace of openness and surrender, even the little things of life become signs of God's wonderful love.

Gratitude:
The Language of Surrender

The German philosopher Martin Heidegger described in his writings an intimate relationship between thinking and thanking. To *think* is to be aware of all that exists; it is to be thought*ful*. To be thought*ful* is to be thank*ful*, realizing that everything is gift, even if things are incomplete, slightly worn, or just plain humdrum. The thoughtful person is one who lives in receptivity, in surrender, to the giftedness of everyday life. Gratitude is the language of surrender because it is spoken from the heart of one who realizes that everything in life bears its own beauty; everything has its own goodness.

The Hebrew term for gratitude is *hikarat hatov,* which means, literally, "recognizing the good." Practicing gratitude means recognizing the good that is already yours. Francis of Assisi was a person of gratitude who thanked God for everything, including God himself. He thanked God for sending Jesus Christ, for the gift of salvation, for the poor, the weak, the lepers, even for his own difficulties, which allowed him to practice greater love of God. Too often we become weighed down by our problems and instead of living in gratitude and surrender, we live in resistance. We become protective of what we have and fight for we don't have or think we should have. Instead of living in the harmony of surrender, we live in the division of resistance. We become neither thought*ful* nor thank*ful*. We lose sight of the fact that gratitude is not an idea but a way of being in the world.

A story about the famous violinist Itzhak Perlman speaks of gratitude and surrender. One evening Perlman was in New York for a concert. As a child he had polio and as a result he wore braces on both legs and walked with two crutches. Needless to say, getting on stage was very difficult for him but as the curtain opened that evening, Perlman entered on stage. The audience applauded and then waited respectfully as he painfully crossed the stage until he reached his chair. He took his seat, signaled to the conductor, and began to play. No sooner had he finished the first few bars than one of the strings on his violin snapped with a sound like a gunshot. Perlman was close enough to the beginning of the piece that it would have been reasonable to bring the concert to a halt while he replaced the string and began again. Instead, he waited a moment and then signaled the conductor to pick up just where they had left off. With only three strings with which to play his soloist part, Perlman continued the piece. He was able to find some of the missing notes on adjoining strings, but where that wasn't possible, he rearranged the music in his head so that it all still held together. He played with passion and artistry, spontaneously rearranging the symphony right through to the end. When he finally rested his bow, the audience sat for a moment in stunned silence. Then they rose to their feet and cheered wildly. They knew they had just witnessed an extraordinary display of human skill and ingenuity. Perlman raised his bow to signal for quiet. "You know," he said, "sometimes it is the artist's task to find out how much beautiful music you can still make with what you have left."[55] He was speaking of the broken string, but his words may also have reflected his own difficult life.

   This story speaks to us of gratitude and surrender because it speaks to us of one person's thoughtfulness in a difficult situation—thankful for what he had to work with. Perlman was able to turn what could have been a dreadful moment into a moment of artistic beauty, even without a full set of strings. Too often we are waiting until everything is right and perfect, and we place high demands on ourselves and others. Instead of living with gratitude, we live with anger and frustration. We lose sight of God's humble love, and we lost sight of ourselves as gifted with love. Gratitude expands the heart to receive each moment of life, however it unfolds, with graciousness and wonder. All is gift freely given, and because life is gift, it is to be graciously received and shared—even sometimes if the strings are broken.

Reflection Questions

- Do I live with gratitude for all that exists, or do I resent the difficulties of my life?
- Do I control every situation, or am I am open to the grace of surrender?
- Do I miss out on the big picture of God's love because I fail to see that love in the everyday blessings of life?

REFLECTIONS

Eighth Evening

Tides of Love

We humans struggle to live in the will of God primarily because we are equipped with intellect and will; we struggle between control of self and desire for God. The power of human intelligence and desire can both lead us to God and prevent us from knowing God. We live in the in-between, suspended between two poles of desire: the desire for the self and the desire for God. We could say surrender is letting go of the egocentric self that covets the true self and hanging on tightly to the desire for God.

Perhaps God knew from the beginning that we humans would struggle to live in the divine good. God did create us gradually, taking time to attend to the details that make up life, making it possible to dwell in a world of created natural beauty where death and surrender are part of everyday life. Nature can teach us the art of surrender because nature is the book of God. Take for example, the small oak tree in our backyard. We just finished a long, cold winter here in Washington, D.C., and the trees persevered despite the frost and cold. The barrenness of their winding limbs was so acute at one point that it seemed like death had consumed all their beauty. One small tree in particular appeared to have met its fate of death. We were sad that a tree so young and fragile did not survive the winter. But winter gave way to spring and the warmth of the sun began to heat the earth, and soon new buds sprouted on the surrounding dome of trees. One day I noticed that the small barren tree also had buds on it. Death had given way to life. Now as spring flows into summer, this small tree is blossoming into fullness.

There is a constancy in nature, an ebb and flow, like the waves of the ocean that throw themselves onto the shore and recede in the giving. Created life is gift and receptivity. It is precisely in the gift of being that nature reveals God's involved goodness. True being is not static or self-enclosed nor does it thrive on control and power; rather, it exists in the constant dynamic movement of self-gift and receptivity. As being gives itself to another, it also receives from the other. Nature mirrors the life of God. In the lives of trees and flowers and oceans and rivers, God can be most Godlike because here the surrender of life unto death yields to the fullness of life.

The entire natural household of God's creation moves like a dance—forward, backward, side to side—bending at times to the forces of nature but never yielding to the power of death. Season after season life continues to emerge with new growth and new beauty in the dappled art of God's creation. In the rhythmic cycle of winter, spring, summer, and fall, trees and flowers and creatures of the earth patiently await life and new life as God surrenders himself in love and life unfolds.

The world of nature is most Godlike because God can express divine love without manipulation or control. From the world of nature we learn simple lessons: be who you are, give of yourself for the sake of the whole, receive without demands, and do not be afraid to die because death is not the end but the beginning of new life.

Give and it shall be given to you, an abundance of overflowing life. Leaves from your life will fall and sometimes you will be crushed underfoot, but if you remain open to God (who continuously surrenders to you in love) life will be yours, an abundance of life beyond what you can ever purchase or possess or control.

Peace (or Moments of Heaven)

If we want to know what it means to do or live in the will of God, we have only to look at a tree or flower by the roadside. A tree does the will of God simply by being a tree, and a flower bears witness to the holiness of God by the uniqueness of its beauty. We humans, on the other hand, tend to complicate the will of God. We make it into a problem to be solved, a riddle of divine-human relations—an impossible task to achieve. We have such a difficult time being ourselves (seldom knowing what this means) or accepting ourselves (because we always want to be someone else) that we would find life as a tree or a flower too difficult for any length of time. We cannot stand still for two minutes without wanting to be something else or needing something else or preoccupied in thought other than the present moment of awareness of our being. Human life depends on movement. Life changes, vacillates, progresses, or regresses depending on our choices. Because humans have so many options from which to choose, we have more difficulty living with an awareness of the will of God or rather to live in the surrender of divine love. If we could be still for two minutes in the surrender of the moment, we might know or better might live in the will of God.

A Jewish tale recounts the story of a young man who sought a famous rabbi to ask about the way to God. Approaching the old, wise figure of the rabbi, the young man asked, "What is the way to God?" The rabbi looked up from his work and answered: "There is no way to God, for God is not other than here and now. The truth you seek is not hidden from you; you are hiding from it."[56] Our search for God's will is in some way the search for our true being. It is not that God hides from us; it is that we hide from ourselves. The less we can face ourselves, the less we can find God and the more difficult it is to know the will of God. To live in our own skin, in the unique being that we are created to be, is to live in the will of God. Nothing further is needed.

Living in the will of God is the true meaning of heaven. Heaven is not a place but a relationship of love. It is not a future reward for a good earthly life; rather, it is the other side of earthly life when we surrender in love to God. Francis of Assisi described heaven as an indwelling in love: "enlightening us to know, for You, Lord, are light; inflaming us to love, for You, Lord, are love; dwelling in us and filling us with happiness."[57] The person who has made a place within his or her heart for God to dwell, who lives in openness and receptivity, who has let go of the reins of control and power, such a person may experience heaven here and now. The momentary experience of abundant peace or joy or goodness is a taste of heaven, where love (within the human heart) is set in order like a homecoming for one's beloved, where light shines brilliantly even if it seems dark to others and where, for a moment, every being is allowed to be itself and, in being itself, an overflow of love is revealed. Heaven is an indwelling in love, and it begins now when we remove the blinders and barriers that prevent us from accepting a God of humble love into our lives and surrendering ourselves into the arms of the One we desire.

Reflection Questions

- What is the primary force in my life, God or my selfish needs?
- What do I find difficult about trust?
- Am I willing to surrender to God, and how does that influence my daily life?
- What do I hold on to in my relationship with God and others? Am I a person of power, and how do I use power?

REFLECTIONS

REFLECTIONS

Ninth Evening

Freedom
in Faith

The secret of nature tells us that one does not do the will of God as if doing a job or accomplishing a task; rather, one lives in the will of God as a way of life. The will of God is the fundamental meaning of our lives here on earth. As we grow in understanding the will of God as the love of God, we let go of the expectations and demands we usually place on ourselves and allow ourselves to stand open in creation, vulnerable to the movements of love. We "let go and let God," allowing God to rule our hearts, occupy our thoughts, and influence our actions. We grow in unity with God, a daily oneness in heart and mind, to the degree that we become possessed by God. "It is no longer I who live, but it is Christ who lives in me," Saint Paul wrote (Galatians 2:20). We may still have our moments of anger or upset or maybe even days of desolation, but now we live with a capacity for wonder and in the generosity of love because we live in receptivity and gratitude for the gift of life bubbling over with the love of God.

The finitude of life continues to show itself in the death of friends, in the financial constraints of modern life, in the decline of health, but possessed by God we live with an inner sense that God is with us and will not leave us orphans or widows. We know, not with the head but with the heart, that the love of God is stronger than death. Indeed, it is God's love that can transform what is dead into life. Possessed by God we live as those who have received an awesome gift freely given, a prize won by sheer fortune. Amazed by this gift, we want to share it with others. Hence, we go out to others—to our neighbors, the poor, the elderly, the stranger—and in sharing of this love, we see God in the extraordinary ordinariness of life. We see that the God who dwells within us also dwells in other people. We realize there is one God and we are one people, one Adam, one Christ.

Possessed by God our eyes are open to our nakedness, our sheer humanity, stripped of its outer garments of power and possessions that hide us in our true being. As we see, so do we love, and as we love, we share in the generation of the divine Word flowing out of the heart of the divine Father. We become partakers of the holy Trinity.

Possessed by God we not only live God's desire for us but we share in the fullness of life. We live in the gift of God's love and hence we live in gratitude. The great doctor of the Church, Saint Irenaeus of Lyons, said "the glory of God is the human person fully alive." The human person fully alive lives not as a "god," but as God's—as one possessed by divine love and filled with grace.[58]

Possessed by God we are fully alive when we can love freely and act justly with no expectations or unnecessary demands but the condition of love itself. The will of God no longer looms over us as something to pursue; rather, the will of God becomes our life wherever we are or whatever we are doing. To live in the will of God as the freedom of love means there is no "right" or "wrong" way to live in God's love. God's will is not primarily a matter of entering religious life or getting married; it does not depend on how one prays or where one prays. Rather as David Brenner writes, "God's will is that you become the person that from eternity you were destined to be—your true self-in-Christ. God's will is that you discover the fullness of life that is uniquely possible in surrendering to divine love and taking up your calling in the kingdom of God."[59] God desires our heart and our happiness, not blind obedience, inexorable suffering, or simple endurance. God desires that we live in the freedom of love. But do we desire this freedom of love as well?

Life in the Spirit

Life in God is life in the Spirit. It is the Spirit within us who makes us cry out, "Abba! Father!" The Spirit of love who breathes forth between the Father and Son, the Spirit who hovers over creation luring it into new things, is this same Spirit who desires to dwell within us and breathe within us. The Spirit of God is the spirit of life, and it is the Spirit who draws us to seek the fullness of life in God. To live in the will of God is to live in the Spirit of God. It is to become a dwelling place for the Spirit because where the Spirit is, so too dwells the Word/Son and Father. Life in God begins in the outpouring of the Spirit, the fire of love, sent into our lives. If we refuse the Spirit of God and choose instead the spirit of the world, we choose against God and against the fullness of life.

Francis of Assisi was a Spirit-filled saint. He accented the importance of the Spirit because without the Spirit there is no true following of Christ. He wrote to his brothers that the heart is the dwelling place of the spirit, that is, of an energy or force that influences the activities or movements of the human person. It is the place where the spirit of the Lord struggles with the spirit of the flesh. To enter into this struggle is to undertake a disciplined life. We cannot truly live in the Spirit if we are constantly following the whims of the flesh and its desires for gratification. We must make a choice for God. Francis was a very human person with a penchant for expensive cloths, fine food, and physical relationships. However, his single-minded choice for God impelled him to renounce the things of the world for the things of heaven.

"Strive for the greater gifts," Saint Paul wrote (1 Corinthians

12:31). Are we ambitious for the higher gifts? Do we trust God enough to let go of worldly things in exchange for a deeper life in the Spirit? The problem in today's consumer world is that we want it all. We want God, material wealth, leisure, autonomy, and satisfied private lives. We consume, take it all in, digest it all, and make it our own but rarely do we share our lives with others, except from our material excess. As a result, many people have empty lives, longing for love, relationship, and the fullness of life. Mother Teresa of Calcutta named the problem of our time as a *crisis of love*. She said the greatest poverty of our time is the poverty of love. When she looked at the West, she did not see power, progress, and prosperity; she saw lonesome valleys filled with the brokenhearted, the almost-living. How naïve of us to think that poverty is of material things alone. Yes, it is true that the physical hunger for bread exists in some countries, but in other places where material wealth abounds, people suffer from loneliness, despair, hatred, unworthiness. They feel unlovable, helpless, and hopeless. Mother Teresa noted that in these places, "they have forgotten how to smile, they have forgotten the beauty of the human touch. They are forgetting what is human love."[60]

Contemporary life is busy. We are pulled in multiple directions as though caught in a hurricane, and an entire day goes by without us giving a thought to God or the indwelling Trinity. We need a type of fasting—not of food but of time, consumerism, multitasking—stopping the frenzy and sitting for a quiet moment to attend to where we are, perhaps naming our awareness of the present moment.

God dwells in ordinary time and in ordinary things: the swaying of trees, the chirping of birds, the gentle rain, the elderly neighbor, the homeless person. The Spirit of life pervades us, quietly sketching the new creation through our lives, if we allow the Spirit to take hold of our lives. We begin to become aware of the world around us when we begin to be aware of God within us. The more we are attuned to the presence of God in our lives, the more in touch we are with God in our world. The will of God then becomes not an ominous force to be feared or reckoned with but a luminous thread of love uniting all beings in creation in harmony and peace.

Love and Do What You Will

To live in the will of God is to be free, not free of commitment or responsibility or accountability but *spiritually* free, free to give oneself over to love without counting the cost. One of the greatest Christian writers in the history of the Church, Augustine of Hippo, pondered the relationship between love and freedom. He distinguished between the human capacity for spiritual freedom and actual spiritual freedom. True freedom, he indicated, is willing according to truth and loving what one wills. The deeper one participates in God's life, he indicated, the greater the freedom in loving God. Life in God is the key to freedom.

The will of God should set us free. Does it? I can only speak from my own experience of more than twenty years in religious life. I entered religious life with the sole intention of devoting my life to God. I entered a monastery of discalced Carmelite nuns because it seemed like a sure path to holiness. The monastery was like a "greenhouse" for God. From sunrise to sunset we were told what to do, where to pray, and how to act. Even though I struggled to adapt to the rigorous life of the monastery, my strong will could not entertain any possibility other than a radical monastic life. I even buried my degrees (including a doctorate in pharmacology) under the altar as a sign of my wholehearted commitment. After several years, however, I realized that I had to make a change if I was to enjoy a peaceful and happy life. So I requested a leave and moved into a Franciscan community for a year of discernment (and yes, I took my degrees with me). I eventually joined the Franciscans and found myself returning to school to study theology and to become something that never crossed my mind—a teacher. After finishing my degree in theology, I moved to an area that I never had a desire to live in—Washington, D.C. Through this life's journey I have found that "letting go" of my lofty expectations and trusting in the love of God has led me on a path to freedom.

I have come to realize that it is not we who go to God, but it is God who comes to us to set us free. The more we open ourselves to God by disabling the control factors of our lives, the more God can come to us and dwell within us. Life in God is not only a daring adventure of love but one must bring to this adventure a sense of trust and hope in God's utter faithfulness, a God who says, "I have loved you with an everlasting love" (Jeremiah 31:3).

As I continue my journey, I see that many people—whether religious, married, or single—are not free because they are unable to realize their capacity for love. Although they are unhappy individuals, they remain fixed in their worlds for various reasons: security, companionship, duty, mediocrity. The signal that something is wrong is lack of spiritual energy within the individual or group. A cloud of inertia hangs over them, and they are unable to really enjoy life because they have failed to tend to the fire of the Spirit within them. We see this same cloud of inertia in the institutional Church where rigidity prevents openness to new ideas and new ways of serving God. Instead of accepting the challenges of the present moment, those who live under this cloud of inertia remain fixed in their tiny worlds. They opt to exchange control, security, and comfort for courage in order to enter the mystery of God wherein lies true happiness.

Freedom in God is the fruit of surrender to God, of making God's will one's own. It is the joy and peace of knowing God in Jesus

Christ, the God who has come to us and set us free. Freedom is not "free-from"; rather, it is the outpouring of the Spirit that arises from deep relationship with God. To live in freedom is to be "free-for"— free for God and the things of God. When Augustine wrote, "love and do what you will," he meant that a person united with God acts freely in love, since a person truly in love with God will not choose against God. Would we choose to hurt or offend the one we love? When we love God and set God as a seal on our hearts, then whatever we choose will be God's will for us.

The story of Francis of Assisi and Brother Masseo traveling on a road in Tuscany is a good example. As Francis and Brother Masseo came to a crossroad they wondered which road to take. Masseo worried that they might take the wrong road and get lost. Francis said they would take the road God wanted them to take, and Masseo asked how they would know. Francis commanded Masseo to twirl around until Francis told him to stop. Then Francis asked which way he was facing. When Masseo answered, Francis said that was the way they would follow.[61] Francis had such a tremendous faith in God's unfailing love that he believed God to be in every direction. If we choose a particular direction, we must trust that God will lead us; and if we find ourselves afraid and in darkness, we must turn and choose again, trusting in God's faithful love.

The key to life in God is freedom. If we claim that we love God and are rooted in God then we should be free, and our freedom should show itself in the way we love, act justly, and live in the truth of God who is Creator, Redeemer, and Savior.

Reflection Questions

- Do I live freely in the Spirit? Am I willing to choose for the sake of God's love even if it means surrendering other loves?
- Am I free to commit my life to another? Does commitment make me free, or does it confine me? What do I find difficult about commitment?

REFLECTIONS

REFLECTIONS

Tenth Evening

Alive in Christ

If love is the key to freedom, then the more purely we love (that is, love without expectations or conditions), the more we are free. Spiritual freedom does not show itself in autonomy or independence but in commitment. Love is relational and the deeper one's love, the more one is committed to the beloved.

Indeed, only when we are free to love can we really commit ourselves wholeheartedly to the other with no other reason than the good of the beloved. True commitment can never arise from a rule or a contract or a duty or an obligation. If we live in a community or exist in a relationship because of duty or contract alone, we exist in a kind of death that manifests itself by "dragging through life," as if we are carrying the weight of the world on our shoulders. Such existence does not reflect the will of God because it quenches the life of the Spirit. "The letter [of the law] kills," according to Paul, "but the Spirit gives life" (2 Corinthians 3:6). How many times we read in the Gospels of Jesus' fidelity to the Spirit of God in contradiction to the letter of Jewish law (for example, eating meat, picking corn on the Sabbath).

Jesus' commitment was to the will of the Father and nothing other. He was so filled with the Holy Spirit that love of the Father and the unfolding of the reign of God dominated his life. Nothing else really mattered. The profound God-centeredness of Jesus' life impelled him to commit his life to the Father even unto death. The freedom of Jesus' life therefore was shown in his fidelity to the Father—in love—unto death. He was not compelled to change his course of action either by the opposing Jews, by the need to conform to his society, or by his disciples. He acted out of the deep well of love within him.

Like Jesus, we see the great reformers of history, even in our own time, such as Martin Luther King, Jr., Dorothy Day, or Oscar Romero, who acted out of a deep inner sense of love and commitment. Their lives show us that the more deeply we root ourselves in the love of God, the freer we are to give ourselves over entirely to the reign of God. This is the heart of the spiritual journey. It is to root one's life not in the center of comfort, cultural acceptance, companionship, or security but in God. It is to live on the margins where we often abandon God, among the less fortunate and misunderstood. To be committed to love and live freely in love is to live on the edge of life where the horizon of a new future struggles to break in. It is to hand oneself over to another even unto death.

Several years ago I taught a course on peace and met a number of dedicated lay women and men involved in peacemaking. I was particularly inspired by one student, Scott Wright, who went to serve the people of El Salvador as a catechist in the early 1980s. When the civil war broke out, he had a chance to leave El Salvador and return to the United States; however, he told me he did not have the heart to abandon the poor and chose to stay with the people in their flight from persecution. What he endured among the poor of El Salvador, including near death by a firing squad, was nothing short of a living witness to the Gospel call of love unto death. By the grace of God he survived the persecution and eventually returned to the States. Today he is married with a small child and his family is truly a Christian witness to peace and justice. The example of this committed Christian shows us that where there is love and freedom, there is the Spirit, and where there is the Spirit, there is life. From the ashes of history new life can emerge if love remains at the center.

Letting Go

Living in the will of God is living in the freedom of love. As Jesus was preparing his disciples for mission he said to them, "If you continue in my word...you will know the truth, and the truth will make you free" (John 8:31-32). Perhaps the key to living freely in the will of God is given in Jesus' words: "If you continue in my word." Too often we keep the Word of God at a comfortable distance from us; we do not allow it to invade our lives and change us. We keep the Word of God at a safe distance by allowing it to be a dead letter rather than a living Word of life. But the Word of God, the words of Scripture, are words of spirit and life—they are meant to instill new life in us, and where there is life, there is change and growth.

Among the ancients the spoken word was an empowered event, one that connoted some type of praxis. For the desert fathers the spoken word of the Abba imparted action and direction to the disciple's life.[62] How many of us have heard the famous story recounted from the desert tradition in which Abba Lot went to see Abba Joseph and told him that he was doing all the right things—fasting, praying and meditating, living in peace and purity of heart—yet it was not enough. He still felt lukewarm, a certain ambivalence in his spiritual life. Whereupon the old Abba Joseph stood up, removed his loincloth, and stretched out his hands toward heaven. His fingers became like ten lamps of fire and he said to him, "if you will, you can become all flame."[63] Letting go of everything that hinders us or separates us from the love of Christ, including our thoughts, our actions, even the way we pray, is the real beginning of life in God. If we allow ourselves to be consumed by love we will become living flames of love.

Of what use is it to pray and do good without being transformed? Of what use is it to hear the Word of God and not make it one's own? Life in God is meant to be transforming, changing us from virtue to virtue and glory to glory (see 2 Corinthians 3:18). If the Word of God is not made our own, then the Scriptures have no more meaning than reading a good novel or the Sunday paper. The Word of God is meant to be taken into one's life, consumed and digested to stimulate growth. We should grow into the freedom of love that God is. We should grow into "another Christ" renewing in our lives the mystery of divine love. Perhaps the will of God remains a question for many of us because we never get beyond the initial stage of knowing God. We never make the Word of God our own; hence, we never really come to know the truth of Christ nor are we set free. We remain enslaved to our selfish desires and material things, marginally Christian but never fully engaged in the life to which we are called. God remains a personal devotion but not the animating center of our lives. Hence the will of God continues to haunt us, especially as we ponder our destiny.

Jesus said to his disciples, "I came to bring fire to the earth, and how I wish it were already kindled!" (Luke 12:49). As Christians we are to set the world ablaze with love, a love that radiates from the depths of our inner lives. We are to be cocreators in Christ. All that we hope for in this world cannot be realized without our transformation and participation. If we truly seek the will of God, then we must seek the path of love that will lead us to truth and from truth to freedom. Only when we are truly free will we hand ourselves over to the fire of love that purges our thick layers of selfishness and transforms us into another Christ. Then will we be able to call ourselves *Christian* and really mean what we say.

Creating the Reign of God

By now it should be clear that the will of God is not like a personal, private Medicare-type plan that ensures safety and happiness for the individual, but the unique love of God planted like a seed in every person created for the reign of God, that is, the unfolding of the Trinity in creation, the communion of all creation in divine love. The will of God is not simply God's love for us, as if the purpose of God is to make us happy. Rather, God loves us for the sake of God—God delights in sharing love and inviting all into the banquet of divine life.

We are not gods but the image of God. Our purpose here on earth is to live in the will of God so that we may give glory to God. There is no other reason to seek the will of God other than for the sake of God. Thus, there is no right or wrong way to live the will of God other than the path that leads to the greatest freedom in love. The question of God's will is not one of "should I" or "shouldn't I" but "am I living freely in love, and is this freedom in love enabling me to live a more godly life?" It is less a question of duty or obligation than attentiveness to a deep inner spirit and commitment to that spirit.

A decision to make a commitment takes time—sometimes a lot of time. Too often we feel compelled to make a choice or decision by family, friends, or community without giving ourselves sufficient time to confirm the direction of the Spirit in our lives. But life in God is a matter of love, not a matter of time. Every moment is an eternal now in which earth becomes a moment of heaven and heaven breaks open here on earth. It is not a question of "what will I do tomorrow or next year" but "what am I doing now, and how am I living in love?"

The fruit of our choice for love shows itself in the way we go about in the world, our contribution to the world, that is, to the unfolding reign of God. Recently I attended a memorial service for a former next-door neighbor, Elodie Hanson, a woman of charm and grace even in her advanced age. She had worked for the Foreign Service for many years and had numerous stories of her travels and adventures. What stood out in recounting her life, however, was her incredible gift of extraordinary love done in ordinary ways. She welcomed every new person to the building as if he or she was of royalty. She invited strangers to dinner and prepared an elegant meal as if every person was famous. One person recounted her first dinner with Elodie, saying that it had a transformative effect on her. She was treated like a queen and never forgot the kindness shown to her. In turn, Elodie responded to every act of kindness with a personal note written in a flowery language of overflowing gratitude. Her attentive acts of love made an extraordinary difference in people's lives. In her own way, she helped create the reign of God.

Interestingly, most of the lives Elodie touched were Catholic religious women who lived in the apartment building. Although she herself was a devout Protestant, she became friends with many of the sisters, often inviting them to dinner. In her own way, she became like the sisters, striving to live the Gospel by making Christ visible to those around her. Her life indicates that freedom in love is infectious and contagious. It can infiltrate and affect any status quo.

Too often we are stifled in love, afraid to be ourselves and reach out to others. We become too preoccupied with ourselves, entangled in our thoughts and feelings, overly concerned about what others might think of us. Real love is subversive because it lives in truth and therefore is not afraid to confront what is false or evil.

Jesus shows us how to live in love and how freedom in love creates the reign of God. Since love always seeks the good of the beloved, true love will often lead us into paths unknown and perhaps journeys of risk or death. Jesus lived in obedience to love of the Father, and this path of love led to the cross. Yet, through the cross new life was poured out for the world.

If we desire to see the reign of God, then we must help create this reign of God by filling the vessels of our lives with the Spirit of love, reaching out to the stranger, challenging corrupt systems, and risking the security and comfort of privatism. Love has the power to transform and the power of transforming love lies within us, for each of us has the power to make present the living God.

Beatrice Bruteau speaks of a transcendent center of freedom within the human person, that is, a freedom to act that arises out of the spontaneous energy of love. She writes, "To enter by our transcendent freedom into Christ and to become a New Creation means to enter by faith into the future of every person and into the very heart of creativity itself, into the future of God."[64] To live in the will of God is to live in the transcendent freedom of love. It is from this center that the reign of God is created by us, that is, from a center of love or energy within us that seeks neither reward nor recompense but flows out of us like an unstoppable fountain because God is its source. It is an overflow of prayer, oneness with God, joy and peace in the Spirit. It is *this* love that helps creates the reign of God.

The Will to Live

When all is said and done about the will of God, it really comes down to one thing: the will to live. As I have tried to emphasize in this book, the will of God is not a blueprint for life but the life I live if I choose the path of love, the path of God each day. To seek the will of God is to ask the following questions: "Am I a person of joy, freedom, creativity, peace, generosity, and kindness?" "Does my existence on this earth contribute to the welfare of the earth and God's people?" "Is Christ alive in this world because of me?" "Does God's Spirit breathe in me more freely because of my choices?"

God's will is God's love, and love is the core of life. Without love, life falls apart. That is why to seek the will of God is ultimately to seek life. Life unfolds in creative engagement with others and in the exchange of goodness. When we seek the will of God, we seek it not for ourselves alone (as if it is "all about me") but we seek it for the sake of others as well, that through our lives God may shine through more luminously in the engagement with others so that others in turn may love more deeply. So there is no right or wrong way to the will of God because it is the path to life, a way of being of God, in God, and for God.

The opposite of life is not death but nothingness, for death itself is an integral part of life; indeed, it may be the very essence of life. Nothingness is defined by death, however, when it involves not the termination of earthly life (although this is the common meaning of death) but the extinction of the Spirit. To be dead is not to breathe. The life of the Spirit that animates our lives and gives them personality goes out of us. Death can happen to any one, at any place, and at any time. It can affect young people, as well as the middle-aged and elderly. It can extinguish married couples, single people, religious men and women, and religious communities. Spiritual death, which is the type of death I am talking about, the death that is nothingness, results when we stop seeking the will of God, when we throw up our hands and say "I give up." Conflict undoubtedly infiltrates human relationships and shows itself in hurt, misunderstanding, distrust, anger, and resentment. It is not that conflict happens; it is what we do when it happens.

To live in the will of God is to live in the constancy of love, even in the midst of conflict and misunderstanding. As long as the Spirit of love dwells within us, we remain on the path of life. When we extinguish the Spirit of love by the power of anger and resentment, we choose against the will of God. We choose spiritual death over life. We may look like we are alive, and biologically we are; however, we have killed the Spirit of life within us by refusing the path of Christ, the path of mercy, compassion, and forgiveness.

I knew a religious sister who lived her life under a dark and brooding cloud. She had experienced deep hurts in the past but never found a way to let them go and allow the goodness of life to prevail. Although she was pleasant to meet on an introductory level and extended herself kindly to others, it was only in living with her that one realized the depth of anger within her. At times she was so self-focused that the will of God seemed irrelevant to her (as did other people). The only thing that mattered was her view of justice. She struggled between the desire to love in freedom and the wounded ego that found it difficult to let go of the past.

Nearby the convent was a middle-aged couple who used to help the sisters from time to time, although they would not attend any services in the church. They too lived beneath a cloud of sorrow and deep hurt, as they had lost their only son in a motorcycle accident many years before. They could not move beyond the tragedy and blamed God (and the Church) for their misfortune. Although they did many kind deeds for the sisters, they harbored a grudge and spoke of spiritual things with a note of bitterness. They were caught between the desire for good and the tragic evil of human failure. When I tried to broach the subject of God's will with them, it almost always turned into a gloom-and-doom discussion. I believe deep down inside they realized that to seek the will of God would be to seek forgiveness, and they could not trust the love of God sufficiently in their lives to embrace the power of forgiveness.

In the Gospel of John, Jesus indicates to his disciples that following the Good Shepherd will mean confronting thieves and brigands but those who truly seek life will not stray. "I came that they may have life," he said "and have it abundantly" (John 10:10). To follow Christ is to be on the way to the fullness of life, to live in the Spirit, to dwell in love. To lose sight of Christ is to fall into the trap of those who try to plunder life. We are created for love. Jesus shows us that the way to love passes through the cross and into the glory of God. Any other way is simply not the path of true humanity and thus does not lead to what we are created for.

If we truly desire to live in the will of God, then we must choose life and the path of life that leads to freedom in love. We may be able to do this in our existing relationships including family or community or we may have to risk and step out in grace, knowing that God's faithfulness in love never fails. Whatever way allows us to live God's will in the fullest way is the way of life for us. We must be open to this way—open to the love of God—so that God's love may take root within us and grow into the freedom of who we are created to be as human persons. Anything we have stored up for ourselves, such as anger, resentment, jealousy, hate, envy, or pride, must be let go for they are the weeds among the wheat of our goodness. If we are extinguishing the Spirit in our lives because we refuse to let go, then we must seek forgiveness. Can we allow the good to triumph over the evil within us? Perhaps the first person we must forgive is our own self because we allow the tenacious claws of our heart to hold onto and cling to deadly attitudes and behaviors. Then we must forgive our enemies and those who have injured us, entrusting them to God's mercy and compassion. Finally, we must forgive the world we have offended by our smallness and mediocrity and refusal to love. Forgiveness is the basis of peace because it is the triumph of love over the divisions of the human heart.

Jesus' desire to do the will of the Father led him to the cross on which he prayed these final words: "Father, forgive them; for they do not know what they are doing" (Luke 23:34). Then he breathed his last, offered up his Spirit, and new life emerged in the universe. We are called to follow this path, for the will of God is the love of God and life feeds on love. If we have failed in love, let us begin anew, for the fullness of life awaits us: "I came that they may have

life, and have it abundantly" (John 10:10), Jesus said. We are promised the fullness of life, and God always keeps a promise.

Reflection Questions

- How does freedom and happiness play out in my following
  Christ? Or do they? Does Christian life lead me to greater
  freedom and happiness? If so, how are these helping me to
  contribute to the unfolding of God's reign?
- If I could imagine the perfect life, what would it look like?
- Am I in love with life, and does this love include God? If so,
  in what ways? If not, why not?

REFLECTIONS

REFLECTIONS

Conclusion

We live in an age that is preoccupied with the perfect life, which is deemed "perfect" by financial success, a well-groomed family, and a successful career. But is material wealth really the perfection of life? On the surface it may seem that way to many people, but for those who have glimpsed the face of God, the perfect life has an entirely different meaning than material wealth. The "perfect life" means living in the generosity of love, the ability to receive love, and to love freely without counting the cost. This type of perfection reflects the glory of heaven. The problem today is that the first type of perfection—material success—often keeps God at a distance because it is a perfection based entirely on human effort, ingenuity, and success. For those who pursue this path, God's will is either another goal to attain or irrelevant; God is enclosed in heaven. For those who pursue the life of perfect love, however, God's will is less a question of "should I?" or "shouldn't I?" than openness to the fullness of love. God's will is not a matter of "doing" but of "being." It is not a work to be accomplished but a way of living in relationship with a God of overflowing love. The one who knows the heart of God knows the will of God, for the will of God is the heart of God aflame with love, a love that desires our healing and wholeness (salvation) so that we may share fully in it.

I have tried to show in this book the integral relationship between the will of God and freedom. Growing in the will of God leads to freedom because it leads us to become ourselves and thus to live without excessive expectations or demands that we often place on ourselves. The more we can discover the love of God as the very center of our lives, the freer we become as we surrender to this love that is the source of our lives.

Freedom is related to truth, as Jesus said, "If you continue in my word...you will know the truth, and the truth will make you free" (John 8:31). To live in the will of God is to live in the truth. It is to accept ourselves and to accept others; it is to acknowledge that we are loved by God and, hence, lovable; and others too are loved by God and also lovable. The truth is that God is with us, within us, and thus we cannot escape the presence of God. We can try to pretend we are "gods," powerful and controlling of our lives, or we can ignore the demands of love that a life in God calls for; but truth, like the will of God, sets us free. If we live in the truth of who we are, we will live in the will of God and in this will is our freedom, regardless of our life circumstances. This does not mean, however, that every situation is to be blindly accepted. To discern every situation is to look at it through the eyes of truth and freedom and ask, "Is my heart centered in this relationship or situation? Is my life at peace in this situation or relationship, filled with hope and goodness?" The will of God means to live in the truthful moments of our lives because God is truth and love feeds on truth.

The problem with the will of God, if indeed a problem does exist, rests within *us*. Too often we complicate God and form the simplicity of God's love into an image of our own expectations or fears. God becomes a ruthless judge, a despot, or like a stern father—none of which are true to the revelation of God as love. It is most difficult for us to accept the plain fact that God is absolute and unconditional love. This fact does not diminish human frailty nor does it erase the tragic side of creation; it simply means that God's love is beyond human comprehension and sustains all that exists. To live in the will of God is to surrender to this incomprehensible love, to realize that heaven knocks on our door, that divine love bends low in surrender to us and invites us into union. Perhaps this is what it means to discern the will of God—not to ask "Is this the right way or the wrong way?" but to ask "Am I ready to accept a God of humble love into my life and to live in the truth of love each day? Can I let go of my own expectations and assumptions and follow the demands of love? Do I listen to the voice of the Spirit that speaks deep within my heart?" Whatever way leads you to respond in truth and freedom—the voice of your heart—this is the will of God for you.

Notes

1. Augustine, *The Confessions of St. Augustine*, trans. and intro. John K. Ryan (New York: Image Books, 1960), 84.

2. Bonaventure, *Itinerarium Mentis in Deum* 1.1., English trans. Ewert Cousins, in Bonaventure: *The Soul's Journey into God, The Tree of Life, The Major Life of Saint Francis* (New York: Paulist, 1980), 59–60.

3. Thomas Merton, *New Seeds of Contemplation* (New York: New Direction Books, 1961), 15.

4. Walter J. Ciszek with Daniel Flaherty, *He Leadeth Me* (New York: Image Books, 1973), 24–25.

5. Ciszek, *He Leadeth Me*, 24.

6. Merton, *New Seeds of Contemplation*, 29–31.

7. See Paul R. Sponheim, "The God of Prayer," in *A Primer on Prayer*, ed. Paul R. Sponheim (Philadelphia: Fortress Press, 1988), 64.

8. *The Confessions of St. Augustine*, trans. John K. Ryan.

9. Bonaventure, *Soliloquium (Solil.)* 1.5 (VIII, 31), English trans. Jose de Vinck, "Soliloquy," in *The Works of Bonaventure*, vol. 3, *Opuscula* (Paterson, NJ: St. Anthony Guild Press, 1966), 44.

10. Merton, *New Seeds of Contemplation*, 14.

11. Ibid., 16–17.

12. Nikos Kazantzakis, Report to Greco, trans. P. A. Bien (New York: Simon and Schuster, 1965), 222–23. Reprinted with the permission of Simon & Schuster Adult Publishing Group from REPORT TO GRECO by Nikos Kazantzakis. Translated from the Greek by P.A. Bien. English translation Copyright © 1965 by Simon & Schuster, Inc. Copyright renewed © 1993 by Helen N. Kazantzakis

13. Kazantzakis, *Report to Greco*, 45.

14. Ronald Rolheiser, *The Shattered Lantern: Rediscovering a Felt Presence of God* (New York: Crossroad, 2001), 104.

15. Barbara Fiand, *Refocusing the Vision: Religious Life into the Future* (New York: Crossroad, 2001), 170–71.

16. Fiand, *Refocusing the Vision*, 176–80.

17. Benedict, *RB 1980: The Rule of Saint Benedict in Latin and English* with notes, ed. Timothy Fry (Collegeville, MN: Liturgical Press, 1981), 157.

18. Thelma Steiger, "Letter from a Hermitage." Personal communication.

19. Timothy Johnson, "Speak Lord, Your Servant Is Listening": Obedience and Prayer in Franciscan Spirituality," *The Cord* 42 (1992): 36–45.

20. Thomas of Celano, "The Remembrance of the Desire of a Soul," 5 in " in *Francis of Assisi: Early Documents*, vol. 2, *The Saint*, ed. Regis J. Armstrong, J. A. Wayne Hellmann, and William J. Short (New York: New City Press, 1999), 248. (Hereafter referred to as FA:EDII followed by page numbers.)

21. Michael Hubaut, "Christ, Our Joy," trans. Paul Barrett. *Greyfriars Review* 9 (Supplement 1995): 86.

22. Christopher Uhl, *Developing Ecological Consciousness: Pathways to a Sustainable World* (Lanham, MD: Rowman & Littlefield, 2004), 239.

23. Cited in Thomas Green, *Weeds Among the Wheat* (Notre Dame, IN: Ave Maria Press, 1984), 41.

24. Green, *Weeds Among the Wheat*, 67.

25. Ignatius of Loyola, *The Spiritual Exercises of St. Ignatius of Loyola*, trans. Elder Mullan, S.J. (New York: P.J. Kenedy & Sons, 1914) (in Second Week; Three Times for Making, in Any One of Them, a Sound and Good Election)

26. Ibid.

27. Ibid. (in Second Week; The First Way to Make a Sound and Good Election).

28. Green, *Weeds Among the Wheat*, 85.

29. Ignatius of Loyola, *Spiritual Exercises* (in Second Week; Three Times for Making, In Any One of Them, A Sound and Good Election).

30. Ibid. (in Second Week; The First Way to Make a Sound and Good Election).

31. In his *Spiritual Exercises* Ignatius tells of picturing and considering "how I shall find myself on the Day of Judgment, to think how I would then want to have deliberated about the present matter, and to take now the rule which I would then wish to have kept, in order that I may then find myself in entire pleasure and joy." Ignatius of Loyola, Spiritual Exercises (in Second Week; The First Way to Make a Sound and Good Election).

32. Green, *Weeds Among the Wheat*, 86.

33. F. Edward Coughlin, introduction to *Writings on the Spiritual Life*, vol. X, *Works of St. Bonaventure*, ed. Robert J. Karris (New York: Franciscan Institute Publications, 2007), 25.

34. Ibid., 28.

35. Bonaventure, "On the Perfection of Life," in *Writings on the Spiritual Life*, 144.

36. Albert Haase, *Swimming in the Sun: Discovering the Lord's Prayer With Francis of Assisi and Thomas Merton* (Cincinnati: St. Anthony Messenger Press, 1993), 119–21.

37. Francis of Assisi, "Letter to Leo" in *Francis of Assisi: Early Documents,* vol. 1, *The Saint,* ed. Regis J. Armstrong, J. A. Wayne Hellmann, and William J. Short (New York: New City Press, 1999), 134. (Hereafter referred to as FA:EDI followed by page numbers.)

38. Haase, *Swimming in the Sun,* 128.

39. Ignatius of Loyola, *Spiritual Exercises,* 115–16.

40. Green, *Weeds Among the Wheat,* 98.

41. Dag Hammarskjold, *Markings,* trans. Leif F. Sjöberg and W. H. Auden (New York: Vintage; Tra edition, 2006),

42. Ignatius of Loyola, *Spiritual Exercises* (in Rules; Rules for Perceiving and Knowing in Some Manner the Different Movements which are Caused in the Soul—The Good, to Receive Them, and the Bad to Reject them and They Are More Proper for the First Week).

43. Ibid.

44. Ibid.

45. Green, *Weeds Among the Wheat,* 145.

46. Francis of Assisi, "Admonition XVI," in FA:EDI, 134.

47. Thomas Merton, *Thoughts in Solitude* (Boston: Shambhala, 1993), 55.

48. *Pseudo-Dionysius: Complete Works,* trans. Colm Lubheid (New York: Paulist, 1987), 287.

49. Bonaventure, "Prologue to the Second Book of Sentences," in *Bonaventure: Mystic of God's Word,* ed. Timothy Johnson (Quincy, IL: Franciscan Press, 1999), 63.

50. Ibid., 60.

51. Vladimir Lossky, *Orthodox Theology,* trans. Ian and Ihita Kesarcodi-Watson (Crestwood, NY: St. Vladimir's Seminary Press, 1978), 73.

52. Kenneth and Michael Himes, "The Sacrament of Creation," *Commonweal* 117 (January 26, 1990): 45.

53. David G. Brenner, *Desiring God's Will* (Downers Grove, IL: InterVarsity Press, 2005), 74.

54. Francis of Assisi, "Earlier Rule" 17.7, in FA:EDI, 75.

55. Alan Morinis, "Gratitude. Path of the Soul 3." www.aish.com/spirituality/growth.www.aish.com/spirituality/growth (accessed April 4, 2008).

56. Cited in Brenner, *Desiring God's Will,* 67.

57. Francis of Assisi, "A Prayer Inspired by the Our Father," in FA:EDI, 158.

58. David Scott, "What's So Special About Mother Teresa?" www.beliefnet.com/story/134/story13413html (accessed April 4, 2008).

59. Brenner, *Desiring God's Will*, 103.

60. Scott, "What's So Special About Mother Teresa?"

61. The Little Flowers of Saint Francis" 11, in *Francis of Assisi: Early Documents*, vol. III, *The Prophet*, eds. Regis J. Armstrong, J. A. Wayne Hellmann, and William B. Short (New York: New City Press, 2001), 584. See also Jane Kopas, "A Franciscan Interpretation of Person in Postmodern Culture," in *Franciscan Identity and Postmodern Culture*, ed. Kathleen A. Warren (New York: The Franciscan Institute, 2003), 67–68.

62. For a good discussion of the power of the word among the desert fathers, see Douglas Burton-Christie, *The Word in the Desert: Scripture and the Quest for Holiness in Early Christian Monasticism* (New York: Oxford University Press, 1993), 107–29.

63. *Sayings of the Desert Fathers: The Alphabetical Collection Joseph of Panephysis* 7, trans. Benedicta Ward (London: Mowbray, 1975), 88.

64. Beatrice Bruteau, *The Grand Option: Personal Transformation and a New Creation* (Notre Dame, IN: University of Notre Dame Press, 2001), 172.